THE BALLAD OF SOAPY SMITH

A Play

by
MICHAEL WELLER

SAMUEL FRENCH, INC.
45 WEST 25TH STREET   NEW YORK 10010
7623 SUNSET BOULEVARD HOLLYWOOD 90046
LONDON   TORONTO

Copyright ©, 1985, by Michael Weller

ALL RIGHTS RESERVED

CAUTION: Professionals and amateurs are hereby warned that THE BALLAD OF SOAPY SMITH is subject to a royalty. It is fully protected under the copyright laws of the United States of America, the British Commonwealth, including Canada, and all other countries of the Copyright Union. All rights, including professional, amateur, motion pictures, recitation, lecturing, public reading, radio broadcasting, television, and the rights of translation into foreign languages are strictly reserved. In its present form the play is dedicated to the reading public only.

THE BALLAD OF SOAPY SMITH may be given stage presentation by amateurs upon payment of a royalty of Sixty Dollars for the first performance, and Forty Dollars for each additional performance, payable one week before the date when the play is given, to Samuel French, Inc., at 45 West 25th Street, New York, N.Y. 10010, or at 7623 Sunset Boulevard, Hollywood, CA. 90046, or to Samuel French (Canada), Ltd. 80 Richmond Street East, Toronto, Ontario, Canada M5C 1P1.

Royalty of the required amount must be paid whether the play is presented for charity or gain and whether or not admission is charged.

Stock royalty quoted on application to Samuel French, Inc.

For all other rights than those stipulated above, apply to Rosenstone / Wender, 3 East 48th Street, New York, N.Y. 10017. In Europe apply to: Michael Imison Playwrights, Ltd., 28 Almeida Street, London N1. 1TD, England.

Particular emphasis is laid on the question of amateur or professional readings, permission and terms for which must be secured in writing from Samuel French, Inc.

Copying from this book in whole or in part is strictly forbidden by law, and the right of performance is not transferable.

Whenever the play is produced the following notice must appear on all programs, printing and advertising for the play: "Produced by special arrangement with Samuel French, Inc."

Due authorship credit must be given on all programs, printing and advertising for the play.

Anyone presenting the play shall not commit or authorize any act or omission by which the copyright of the play or the right to copyright same may be impaired.

No changes shall be made in the play for the purpose of your production unless authorized in writing.

The publication of this play does not imply that it is necessarily available for performance by amateurs or professionals. Amateurs and professionals considering a production are strongly advised in their own interests to apply to Samuel French, Inc., for consent before starting rehearsals, advertising, or booking a theatre or hall.

No part of this book may be reproduced, stored in a retrieval system, or transmitted in any form, by any means, including mechanical, electronic, photocopying, recording, or otherwise, without the prior written permission of the publisher.

ISBN 0 573 61970 0   Printed in U.S.A.

A New York Shakespeare Festival Production/Newman Theater

Joseph Papp
presents

THE BALLAD OF SOAPY SMITH

by
Michael Weller

Directed by
Robert Egan

Scenery by	*Costumes by*	*Lighting by*
Engene Lee	**Robert Blackman**	**Jennifer Tipton**
Music by	*Songs by*	*Fight Direction by*
Norman Durkee	**Michael Weller**	**B.H. Barry**

Hair and Makeup by
Marlies Vallant

with

William H. Andrews	Denis Arndt	Nesbitt Blaisdell
Larry Bryggman	Timothy Carhart	Lori Tan Chinn
Hortensia Colorado	Christopher Cooper	Jon DeVries
James Eckhouse	Pierre Epstein	Annette Helde
James Hilbrandt	Cherry Jones	Olek Krupa
Laura MacDermott	Stephen Markle	Kevin McClarnon
John C. McGinley	Peter McRobbie	Brooke Myers
Marjorie Nelson	E. Claude Richards	Peter Rogan
Jimmy Smits	John Spencer	Brad Sullivan
Kevin Tighe	Dierk Torsek	Joseph Warren
	Marisa Zalabak	

Associate Producer
Jason Steven Cohen

"The Ballad of Soapy Smith" was originally commissioned and produced by
the Seattle Repertory Theatre, Seattle, Washington.

THE BALLAD OF SOAPY SMITH was originally produced by the Seattle Repertory Theatre, Seattle, Washington and opened on October 26, 1983 with the following cast:

Pianoman	Norman Durkee
Man on Boat	James Brousseau
Paul Anthony MacAleer	Christopher Cooper
Tripod Schultz	J. V. Bradley
Jefferson Randolph (Soapy) Smith	Denis Arndt
George Wilder	John Aylward
Frenchie Villiers	Frank Corrado
Major James Strong	Paul Hostetler
William Whitmore	Richard Riehle
Frank Reid	Kevin Tighe
Calvin Barkdull	Scott Caldwell
Michael C. Sherpy	Michael Santo
Kitty Chase	Kate Mulgrew
Mattie Silks	Marjorie Nelson
Burke Gallagher	Ted D'Arms
Charlie (The Reverend) Bowers	Lee Corrigan
William (Doc) Jackson	Mark Jenkins
Syd Dixon	Kurt Beattie
Red Gibbs	Michael J. Smith
Townswomen	Toni Cross, Kathleen Worley
Fritz	Roderick Aird
Reverend Dickey	Clayton Corzatta
Tagish Sam	William P. Ontiveros
Violet	Gretchen Rumbaugh
Pearl	Tina Marie Goff
Jensen	Rod Pilloud
Sick Man in Bed	Corky Dexter
Mollie Fewclothes	Karen Kay Cody
Corporal Egan	Frank Corrado
U.S. District Commissioner Charles A. Sehlbrede	Rod Pilloud
Photographer	James Brousseau
Gov. John Brady of Alaska	Ted D'Arms
J.D. Stewart	Brian Martin

SEATTLE CAST
(continued)

Miners, Skagway Militiamen, Townspeople, Alaska Militiamen, Guards, Mattie's Girls, Vigilantes, Vigilante Wives:

Roderick Aird, James Brousseau, Scott Caldwell, Karen Kay Cody, Frank Corrado, Clayton Corzatte, Toni Cross, Ted D'Arms, Corky Dexter, Tina Marie Goff, Mark Jenkins, Brian Martin, Rod Pilloud, Gretchen Rumbaugh, Michael Santo, Michael J. Smith, Kathleen Worley

Director — Robert Egan
Scenic Designer — Eugene Lee
Costume Designer — Robert Blackman
Lighting Designer — Spencer Mosse
Songs — Michael Weller
Musical Score — Norman Durkee
Sound Designer — Michael Holten

The original New York production of THE BALLAD OF SOAPY SMITH was presented by the New York Shakespeare Festival, produced by Joseph Papp, and opened on November 12, 1984 with the following cast:

Pianolady	Nancy Waldman
Paul Anthony MacAleer	Christopher Cooper
Tripod Schultz	James Hilbrandt
Jefferson Randolph (Soapy) Smith	Denis Arndt
George Wilder	Jon DeVreis
Frenchie Villiers	Jimmy Smits
Major James Strong	William H. Andrews
William Whitmore	Brad Sullivan
Frank Reid	Kevin Tighe
Calvin Barkdull	Larry Bryggman
Michael C. Sherpy	Dierk Torsek
Kitty Chase	Cherry Jones
Mattie Silks	Marjorie Nelson
Burke Gallagher	John Spencer
Charlie (The Reverend) Bowers	Nesbitt Blaisdell
William (Doc) Jackson	Peter McRobbie
Syd Dixon	Stephen Markle
Red Gibbs	Timothy Carhart
Townswomen	Lori Tan Chinn, Hortensia Colorado, Annette Helde, Laura MacDermott, Brooke Myers, Marisa Zalabak
Fritz	Olek Krupa
Reverend Dickey	Pierre Epstein
Tagish Sam	E. Claude Richards
Jensen	Peter Rogan
Sick Man in Bed	James Eckhouse
Mollie Fewclothes	Marisa Zalabak
Corporal Egan	Kevin McClarnon
U.S. District Commissioner Charles A. Sehlbrede	John Spencer
Photographer	James Eckhouse

NEW YORK CAST
(continued)

Gov. John Brady of Alaska. . . . . Joseph Warren
J.D. Stewart. . . . . John C. McGinley
Oriental Woman . . . . Lori Tan Chinn

Miners, Skagway Militiamen, Townspeople,
Alaska Militiamen, Guards, Mattie's Girls,
Vigilantes, Vigilante Wives:

Lori Tan Chinn, Hortensia Colorado, James Eckhouse, Annette Helde, Olek Krupa, Laura MacDermott, Kevin McClarnon, John C. McGinley, Brook Myers, Peter Rogan, Jimmy Smits, Joseph Warren, Marisa Zalabak

Director — Robert Egan
Scenery by — Eugene Lee
Costumes by — Robert Blackman
Lighting by — Jennifer Tipton
Music by — Norman Durkee
Songs by — Michael Weller
Fight Direction — B.H. Barry
Hair and Makeup — Marlies Vallant

THE CAST

PAUL ANTHONY McALEER
TRIPOD SCHULTZ
JEFFERSON RANDOLPH (SOAPY) SMITH
GEORGE WILDER
FRENCHIE VILLIERS
MAJOR JAMES STRONG
FRANK REID
MICHAEL C. SHERPY
WILLIAM WHITMORE
CALVIN BARKDULL
KITTY CHASE
MATTIE SILKS
BURKE GALLAGHER
CHARLIE (THE REVEREND) BOWERS
WILLIAM H. (DOC) JACKSON
SYD DIXON
RED GIBBS
REVEREND DICKEY
FRITZ
TAGISH SAM
JENSEN
MOLLIE FEWCLOTHES
CORPORAL EGAN
COMMISSIONER CHARLES A. SEHLBREDE
GOVERNOR BRADY OF ALASKA

TOWNSPEOPLE, PROSTITUTES, DANCE HALL GIRLS, MILITIAMEN, OTHER VIGILANTES, MRS. DICKEY, MRS. WHITMORE, MRS. BARKDULL, FRANK CLANCY, OTHERS.

With proper doubling this play can be (and has been) performed with a cast of 22.

THE BALLAD OF SOAPY SMITH

ACT ONE
Scene One

PAUL McALEER enters, addresses us.

PAUL. Welcome, friends. My name is Paul Anthony McAleer, farm boy, dreamer, poet ... forgotten. I lived those Klondike years, and I left this behind *(Shows notebook.)* to show for it. What a time it was; a time of wrecklessness, adventure, of fortunes made and lost in the wink of an eye ... a time of golden dreams. So here I am, conjured back from the once-living to tell you all about a man who was the very emblem of those days, a man called Soapy Smith. But this time the truth. The whole truth. I have my reasons, as you'll soon see. *(He opens notebook, dons spectacles, strikes stance and reads out.)*
A CENTURY WAS ENDING
THE WORLD SLEPT UNAWARE
THAT UNDERNEATH ALASKAN SOIL
REPOSED A METAL RARE

THEN ONE SPRING DAY IN '97
FROM OUT THE WILD'NESS CAME

ARGONAUTS WITH GLEAMING EYES
TO STAKE A DOUBLE CLAIM

THEY REACHED INTO THEIR LEATHER POKES
AND WHEN OUT THOSE NUGGETS ROLLED
ONE CRY WAS HEARD ALL ROUND THE WORLD
'HEY BOYS, THE KLONDIKE'S MADE OF GOLD
IT'S MADE OF SOLID GOLD!!!
(He holds up the notebook and announces:) 'The Ballad of Soapy Smith, by Paul Anthony McAleer.'

Scene Two

The Lynn Canal, Alaska. Fog. Rowboat. Aft, a new steamer trunk. Forward, peering into fog ahead, two men: JEFFERSON RANDOLPH (SOAPY) SMITH and GEORGE WILDER. JEFF sits elegantly straight-backed. WILDER huddles miserably in heavy overcoat. TRIPOD, at the oars, sings as he rows.

TRI.
I CAME NORTH WITH A PICK AND SHOVEL
I CAME LOOKING FOR KLONDIKE GOLD
ALL I FOUND IS CARE AND TROUBLE
LOST MY DREAMS IN THE KLONDIKE COLD

LORD, LORD, HEAR MY PRAYER
I'M SO SICK WITH TROUBLE AND CARE
TAKE ME BACK TO MY WIFE AND KIN

AND I'LL NEVER COME NORTH FOR THE GOLD AGAIN...

JEFF. Look at it, Georgie-boy. Sends shivers all up and down your spine, don't it? *(JEFF's accent is courtly-Southern, his manner charming, playful, intimate.)*

WILD. All I see is fog.

JEFF. But somewhere, just the other side of it, Skagway; the pot of gold at the end of the rainbow.

WILD. Looks more like the end of the god damn earth to me.

JEFF. Come on, old grumpus, fortune beckons and life is good, let's see some jubilation.

WILD. Leave me alone, Soapy. I'm tired, I'm hungry, I'm wet and I'm cold, and I wish to hell I never left Colorado, come chasing up here to the middle of god damn Nowhere, Alaska.

JEFF. Now Georgie-boy, all I asked was you stake my operation. The choice of travel was your very own.

WILD. That money was earning interest in a bank. I had investments. Hell, I'm a businessman.

JEFF. You're a hustler, old son. It's in your blood like the color red, so don't start getting all holier-than-thou on me. God gave us a gift, and we must use it to the fullest and celebrate his glory thereby. Just wrap your brain around one word, Georgie-boy: Klondike! Biggest damn news since King Midas grew fingernails.

WILD. Biggest rumor, you mean.

JEFF. You know your trouble? You take everything too serious. Look at me now, easy come, easy go, and in my heart I'm singing all the time.

WILD. That's not what you said when we were run out

of Denver. And that's not what you said when we were run out of Creede. And Houston. And San Francisco, when we nearly got our lights blown out into the bargain.

JEFF. We've had a set-back or two, I don't deny it. But this time we're onto a sure thing. How we doing back there, Mr. Boatman?

TRI. *(looking at water)* Not much current in the canal tonight. Mebbee a little movement ... yay. *(points)*

JEFF. Could you enlighten me as to whether that's a good thing or a bad thing?

TRI. If the tide's coming in, it means Skagway lies yay. *(points)* If it's going out, means Skagway's over there. *(points opposite)* Figure out which way the tide's moving, we got her licked.

JEFF. Time is money, Mr. Boatman, so figure quick and let's get hauling.

TRI. Kind of hard to do when you ain't got a reference. Fog's a right bastard that way.

WILD. Are you saying we're lost out here?

TRI. We're dis-orientied some.

WILD. We paid you good money to get us to Skagway. You're a boatman. Get us there.

TRI. No, sir, never saw salt water till a month ago. Worked the railroad. Don't know how the hell I ended up here. Mystery to me.

JEFF. *(points)* Skagway's over there.

WILD. How do you know?

JEFF. Just a hunch, George. We can't float around out here all night, might as well take a chance. Unless, of course, you prefer the other direction. What's your pleasure, heads or tails?

WILD. Tails.

JEFF. *(Takes coin from pocket.)*
Heads he's a good man
Tails he's a bad
Heads he's a happy man
Tails he's a sad
Heads the Lord's gonna lead him to gold
Tails the Devil's gonna have his soul.
(He flips coin, WILDER catches it. Both look.) Guess it just ain't your day, George. *(points)* There's your course, Mr. Boatman.

WILD. *(checking coin)* Double heads, Jesus, Jeff.

JEFF. You know how it pains me to lose.

TRI. Pardon my noticing, but you fellers don't seem much like prospectors to me.

JEFF. *(turns)* What's on your mind, Mr. Boatman?

TRI. As employment goes, I don't much care for water. Thought I might. I don't. If you ever need a good man, see, just ask around for Schultz, Tripod Schultz, that's me.

WILD. Shhhh ... I hear something.

TRI. Steamer. Sounds like a big 'un.

WILD. Which way?

TRI. Damn echoes. Somewhere in there! And getting closer. AHOY! WHO ARE YOU? WHERE YOU PUTTING IN? CAN YOU HEAR ME???

VOICE. WE'RE THE JENNY RAND OUT OF SAN FRANCISCO. WE'RE BOUND FOR SKAGWAY. ARE YOU IN TROUBLE? DO YOU NEED HELP? AHOY, CAN YOU HEAR ME? WHO ARE YOU??? *(Through this, unseen steamer nears, passes and heads away in the fog. On board we hear sounds of singing, rinky-tink piano, merriment)*

TRI. *(ears cupped, following)* She's headed yay. There's our course.

JEFF. Just where I said. See that, Georgie-boy, I'm telling you, this town's gonna be lucky for me, I can feel it in my blood. *(steamer fading)* Listen to all that carry-on. All of 'em Skagway bound. And behind every voice, a living, breathing human being, all of 'em wearing clothes, clothes with pockets, pockets with wallets. That, old son, is the sound of money in the night, just waiting for a dark hand to reach out and carry it gently away.

WILD. Soapy Smith, you are out of your god damn mind.

JEFF. Colonel Smith, George. Colonel Jefferson Randolph Smith. Don't slip up.

WILD. *(wry salute)* Colonel.

JEFF. Mr. Boatman, follow that beautiful, beautiful noise.

Scene Three

Strong's Miner Supply, Skagway. Night, shutters drawn. Men in hoods and dusters, gathered waiting in light of single kerosene lantern: MAJOR JIM STRONG, WILLIAM WHITMORE, CALVIN BARKDULL, MIKE SHERPY and FRANK REID. Pause. Knock on door. WHITMORE opens it, admitting two men in hoods leading FRENCHIE VILLIERS, gagged and blindfolded, hands tied behind back. They seat him roughly and remove gag and blindfold.

FRENCH. What this is? Why you bring me here?

STRONG. Tell us what happened at the Pack Train Saloon.

FRENCH. Why I must tell you? You are no the law.

WHIT. *(with gun)* You'll tell us all right or I'll blow your head off 'fore you got time to piss out your last whiskey.

FRENCH. *(quickly)* Is no my fault. Russian Johnny, he say I cheat him in the poker game, him and his sonna bitch friends they say that thing.

STRONG. Witnesses say Russian Johnny was unarmed.

FRENCH. Is a lie. They hide his gun after so it can look very bad for me. They are better to stay away from Frenchie Villiers. I cut them all in the neck, phoo!!! *(spits)*

STRONG. Take him out back and wait.

FRENCH. You want money, eh? I have very much. Two thousand dollars, maybe more. You let me go away tonight, I tell you where is hiding, yes? *(Hooded men pull him towards door.)* You can make nothing with me. You are no the law. *(Hooded men knock him out and pull him through door. Others remove hoods, and as scene proceeds, they take off their dusters, revealing themselves as businessmen.)*

WHIT. There you are. He done it, he admits it, we got ourselves a clear case.

REID. We have no authority to deal with this man. It's strictly a matter for the law.

WHIT. Except for one minor problem, Frank Reid. There ain't no law in Skagway. We're it.

SHERPY. No, no, no, there's a U.S. District Commissioner ten miles down the canal in Dyea.

WHIT. That man's a god damn crook and you know it. He'll just take a bribe and let the son of a bitch go free, same as always....

REID. Washington promised us a new commissioner....

WHIT. They been promising for six months. Washington don't give a damn about our problems. Hell, Skagway ain't even a name on the map yet.

STRONG. All right, Bill, so what do we do? We have a murderer on our hands. Now do we ship him out of town? Rough him up? Try to scare him?

WHIT. There's only one thing the criminals in this town will ever understand, and that's one of their own kind hanging dead and stinking from a gallows tree.

STRONG. Bill, we're a Vigilance Committee, not a lynch mob.

WHIT. This town's ours, god damn it. Us, right here in this room. We built it and it's up to us to protect it. Now I vote we hang Frenchie Villiers.

BARK. I second the motion.

STRONG. All right, you two, now steady on. I am the chairman of this committee and we're going to do this thing right....

WHIT. Don't give me none of your 'steady-on' stuff, Jim Strong. I'm gonna show you something to make you sit up and sweat. Calvin, read 'em what you got today, go on, read it.

BARK. *(Takes out folded newspaper and reads aloud.)* San

ACT I   THE BALLAD OF SOAPY SMITH   17

Francisco Examiner, front page. "Klondikers Beware: Our correspondent has recently received reports of rampant lawlessness from the port town of Skagway, Alaska. We therefore advise travellers to the goldfields to avoid this dangerous town and seek other and safer routes into the Klondike."

SHERPY. *(Takes newspaper.)* This is very bad news, gentlemen. If the examiner sees fit to print a story like this, every paper in the country is liable to pick it up.

REID. Didn't I warn you this would happen? But no, you had a clever angle to draw business. Make Skagway an open town, that's what you said. Look the other way when it comes to liquor and gaming and the good-time ladies and we'll all profit by the stampede. Well, it worked, gentlemen. Only now you don't seem to like it.

WHIT. You got something material to add, or you just sticking your shovel in?

REID. I'm reminding you that how we set this town up came back on us. And so will hanging. Sooner or later, we'll pay the price.

WHIT. Well, I'm sure we're all just greatful as hell to our town engineer for his pearls of wisdom, but there's a vote been called for, Jim. Get on with it.

STRONG. All in favor of hanging? *(WHITMORE and BARKDULL raise hands. SHERPY glances at newspaper and raises hand. Pause. STRONG raises hand.)*

REID. Jim....

STRONG. *(Proffers newspaper.)* Read it, Frank. The future of Skagway's at stake here.

WHIT. How do you vote, Frank Reid?

REID. You have your majority. You don't need my vote.

WHIT. Seems like Mr. Reid is trying to place himself out of harm's way.

REID. I swore the oath of loyalty. That stands ... for now. But I won't cast my vote for murder.

WHIT. To hell with him. Let's do it.

STRONG. Give the word. Go home by seperate routes. Don't be seen together. *(Exit all but STRONG and REID.)*

STRONG. I don't like this any better than you do, Frank, believe me.

REID. Then why'd you vote with them? The two of us could have stopped it.

STRONG. You're not a tradesman. You don't understand what's at stake here.

REID. I didn't come North to make money. I came to make a life.

STRONG. Look, Frank, you and me been moving west together enough years to know a town starting up has to make do with its own kind of justice till something better comes along.

REID. Justice isn't a suit of clothes, Jim. You can't just cut it any old way to fit your needs. It's absolute, or it's nothing at all. What's happening tonight is murder. The rest is all talk. *(exit)*

Scene Four

PAUL McALEER, wearing spectacles, notebook in hand, strikes a pose and reads.

PAUL.
PICTURE THIS, TEN THOUSAND STRANGERS
CAST UPON A SHORE
WOODEN SHACKS, MUDDY STREETS
AND HUNGRY DOGS GALORE

NOW PICTURE THIS, A HUSH
THAT RIPPLES THROUGH THIS TEEMING LAND
TEN THOUSAND FACES TURN
AND THERE A MAN IN BLACK DOES STAND
(He closes notebook, addresses us.) When I arrived in Skagway, there were just under four hundred people here. A month later there were ten thousand. It was a seething, roaring madhouse of humanity. In a word, it was everything I ever dreamed of, mankind writ large, living full blown at the very edge of the world. How does it go: Careful what you want in life, you may get it. *(Opens notebook, reads.)*
A STRANGER CAME TO SKAGWAY TOWN
ONE MISTY AUTUMN DAY
SAID HE, 'MY NAME IS COLONEL SMITH
AND I THINK I'VE COME TO STAY.'

MYSTERIOUS HIS ARRIVAL WAS
UNKNOWN HIS ENTERPRISE
AND SECRETS DEEP AS NIGHT DID MOVE
BEHIND HIS SMILING EYES
BEHIND HIS GENTLE, SMILING EYES

Scene Five

JEFF SMITH's Oyster Parlor. Rough and ready place. Steamer trunk sits open, shirts and collars in view. Jeff's suit hangs against wall, hat above on shelf, boots below on floor, like an invisible man. JEFF, in silk smoking jacket, pours coffee for himself and MATTIE SILKS, a woman of uncertain years, dressed with gaudy flair and smoking a cheroot.

JEFF. Fires. Vandalism. Fistfights causing severe damage to property. Terrible accidents can happen in an establishment such as yours. But they simply won't. Not if you accept my offer, that is. Otherwise ... oh, lets not dwell on sullen thoughts. Do you take sugar? It's white.

MATTIE. Just what exactly is it you're peddling, Colonel?

JEFF. As you know if you've been around at all, which I believe you have, and I mean that in the nicest possible way, the going rate for decent protection is one half your gross earnings. But if you sign on now, I'll offer you a special introductory rate of forty percent, plus a very warm spot in my heart for being among the quick. Try the milk, it's dairy fresh.

MATTIE. Forty percent? No deal. My girls barely keep me in cigars as it is.

JEFF. Business may improve.

MATTIE. You talk mighty large for someone who just blew into town.

ACT I   THE BALLAD OF SOAPY SMITH

JEFF. Two nights ago I stepped off the boat. Yesterday I bought me this fine saloon. Today I'm receiving a charming lady caller. Tomorrow, who knows? That's my tempo, ma'am: allegro furioso.

MATTIE. Twenty-five percent. Until I see if there's any fire under all that fancy smoke of yours.

JEFF. Mattie Silks, let me tell you a little something about myself. Never bargain with Jeff Smith. Never question Jeff Smith. And never repeat what Jeff Smith tells you in private. Do take that very much to heart, ma'am. Now enough business-talk, it just gets in the way of friendly chit-chat, and I am so looking forward to you and your girls becoming very special friends of mine, aren't you, Mattie? Is it too soon to call you Mattie?

MATTIE. You are one smooth piece of goods, Colonel Smith.

JEFF. I knew we'd get along just fine.

(Enter BURKE GALLAGHER with gang: CHARLIE 'THE REVEREND' BOWERS, WILLIAM 'DOC' JACKSON, SYD DIXON and RED GIBBS. BURKE is a large convivial Irishman who plays the amiable buffoon to conceal the danger beneath.)

BURKE. *(huge grin)* Colonel Smith, I presume?

JEFF. *(to MATTIE)* So pleasant talking to you, Ma'am. Don't be a stranger, y'hear?

MATTIE. We'll see what we'll see, Colonel Smith. *(exits)*

JEFF. Burke Gallagher, fancy meeting you in Skagway. What brings you North?

BURKE. Same as brings yourself, I'd wager. Drawn, as it were, by the Holy Trinity; chaos, confusion and easy money. When I heard tell of a Colonel Smith buying Clancy's Saloon, a little spark went off in me brain, isn't that right, lads? Could it be, says I to meself, could it be that me old scoundrel the Soapman has sniffed the sweet scent of the Golden Northland at last?

JEFF. Whiskey?

BURKE. I never refuse a wee drop of the critter.

JEFF. *(Indicates trunk.)* Under the clothing. Help yourself.

BURKE. You'll join me?

JEFF. I don't drink.

BURKE. Jesus-Mary-and-Joseph, how could I forget a thing like that. Soapy Smith, ever cool and sober through this Vale of Tears.

JEFF. There's glasses behind the bar.

BURKE. *(Finds bottle in trunk.)* Haig and Haig, two of the finest sons a mother ever loved. *(Looks further.)* What's all this, then? Markers. Faro cloth. Playing cards. Dice. Saints preserve us, a glimpse of paradise. How'd you get all this past the customs boys, if you don't mind me asking?

JEFF. Now you know my business, Burke. What's yours?

BURKE. I've come to bid you welcome, dear heart. Two old friends well met in the wilderness, balm to the weary traveller and so forth.

JEFF. Burke, what the hell is behind all this palaver?

BURKE. *(pause)* Ah, well, truth be told, I'm faced with a terrible dilemma, what with your arrival on the scene and all. In your own immortal words, "Do unto others as they would do unto you, only do it first." As it happens, dear heart, I'm in Skagway before you. Do you see me quandry?

JEFF. You're a card handler, I'm an organiser. You play for me, I protect you. Where's the conflict?

BURKE. Well, you see, I'm expanding my horizons, as it were.

JEFF. You? Running a gang? Get serious, Burke.

BURKE. I'm deadly serious. As you can see, I've already made considerable progress in consolidating some of the finer elements hereabouts.

WILD. *(entering)* Burke Gallagher...!!!

BURKE. Mr. Wilder! Your gun, if you please. *(SYD takes WILDER's gun. BOWERS frisks JEFF.)*

JEFF. Burke has himself a gang now, Georgie-boy. George warned me I'd come to rue the day I saved your life back in Creede. I should pay more attention to George.

BURKE. If you'll be good enough to put your clothes on, my boys'll escort the two of you to a waiting southbound steamer.

JEFF. How'd he scrape together a sorry-looking bunch of deadbeats like you all, anyway? Buy you a few free drinks, did he? Throw around a little danger talk? Did he tell you the one about his Pa? How he shot him dead and cut the mouth off his face? How is it, Burke, you keep it in a jar of alcohol by the bed and laugh yourself to sleep cause you know your old man can't give you any more lip? Did he tell you that one?

BURKE. They seen the jar.

JEFF. Stop this, Burke, or I'll be forced to treat you serious.

BURKE. Get dressed, Jeff. Now. *(to gang)* Check his clothes. The boots as well. There'll be a derringer in the left toe, if memory serves. *(DOC finds it.)*

JEFF. *(Sees he's covered, starts dressing.)* Burke, human intercourse is such a delicate business. Such a world of unspoken understandings at the root of things. Take you and me, for example. *(Snaps finger.)* My tie, if you please. *(BURKE nods, SYD fetches tie.)* Now you are a master card handler, that's a simple fact. And knowing it for true, I concede the field to you, and happily so, without a word being spoken. My waistcoat if you please. *(BURKE again nods, SYD fetches waistcoat.)* But when it comes to the human sciences, let's call 'em: organisation, strategy, public relations and so forth, I'd expect you to recognize my superior gifts in these areas and concede the field to me, don't that seem reasonable?

BURKE. My God, but you are one cool frightening bastard under that smile of yours. The world is full of little holes you can wriggle through sideways, that's what you reckon, ain't it? Well, not this time, dear heart.

JEFF. My coat.

BURKE. Get it yourself.

JEFF. *(obeys)* I'd never move in on a town like this without people I knew and trusted. Skagway's big pickings, and that draws people who play for keeps. No, I'd send my boys in ahead of me to scout the situation before I'd ever dare show my face. Find out who's setting up as the big noise, have 'em infiltrate his gang, gain his trust and confidence and then, when my whole set-up was in place but for the straw man in the middle .... I'd appear.

BURKE. *(Pulls gun.)* That's enough talk. Get your boots on.

JEFF. You're acting jumpy, Burke. If you aim to be a leader of men, you gotta learn to hide the willies. See my hand? Not a tremor. Let's see yours. *(JEFF's hand is out flat, palm down.)*

BURKE. No more, Jeff. I'll use this, don't think I won't.

JEFF. You're not a killer, Burke. At least I hope you're not. Because if I thought so, if I truly believed you could murder the man who saved your life, dear God, I'd nail your nuts to a tree and set the woods on fire.

BURKE. Don't make me do it, Jeff. *(backing away)* I'm letting you go with your life, now we're even, but don't push your luck. Draw your guns, boys. *(Gang obeys. JEFF advancing on BURKE and slowly wrapping his hand around the barrel of BURKE's gun, gripping it fast.)* I'm warning you, Jeff, leave go your hand. *(Pulls trigger ... click.)* What the hell? *(Pulls more ... more clicks.)* What's going on here?

BOWERS. *(Drops a handful of bullets on bar counter.)* We took a few precautions, as instructed, Jeff.

BURKE. *(The penny drops.)* Holy mother o'God....

JEFF. You made a mistake, Burke. Such a bad mistake. You pulled the trigger.

BURKE. *(pause)* No harm done, eh, Jeff? You can't blame a poor fool for seeing the main chance. I'll play cards for you, why I'd be delighted to do that. You can have seventy-five percent, how's that? Hell, I'll make you a pile of money.

JEFF. We have no further business, Mr. Gallagher. You take care of yourself, y' hear? *(BURKE, defeated, exits. Gang jeers him as he goes.)* Pity Burke knows so much. He *was* a good card handler. *(JEFF hands WILDER a gun. WILDER understands and drifts out after BURKE to eliminate a problem.)*

SYD. Jeff, you old scoundrel, what took you so long...???

DOC. We were wondering if you'd ever get here...

BOWERS. Good to see your sinful mug again, Soapy!

JEFF. I am Colonel Jefferson Randolph Smith, and don't you forget it. Now who the hell are you boys? I don't believe I've had the pleasure.

BOWERS. Reverend Charles Bowers at your service, Colonel. Congregationalist, itinerant by calling, here to spread the gospel along the trail in-country...

ALL. ...praise God...

BOWERS. ...Amen.

DOC. *(Comes forward.)* Doctor William Jackson, doing field research on the containment of cholera in overcrowded populations. *(handshake)* Masons?

JEFF. Houston, Lodge 4.

DOC. Columbus, Lodge 21.

JEFF. Good, Doc, very good.

SYD. Sydney Dixon, Colonel, on a recreational tour of the Territories, strictly pleasure, but with an eye on financial opportunities for certain European speculators.

JEFF. Forget the Europe part, Syd. That plays fine back in the States, but up here it smells un-patriotic. Mr. Gibbs?

RED. Billy Gibbs, Colonel. My friends call me 'Red.'

I'm a ships outfitter, been saving up to send for my dear old Ma, who's ailing back in Braintree, Massachussetts....

JEFF. Don't lay it on so thick, Red. Your face is your trump card.

(Two gunshots offstage. Gang remove hats, BOWERS makes sign of the cross, etc.)

JEFF. Sorry for the delay, fellers, we were double checking some other towns along the coast. Skagway still looks like number one, what do you think?

DOC. It's perfect, Jeff. The town's growing like brushfire. Nine, ten thousand strangers piled up here waiting to get through the pass, and more arriving daily...

SYD. ...All of 'em green as grass, you could hustle 'em in your sleep.

JEFF. Any law?

DOC. A few Vigilantes. Hard to pin 'em down, but they don't look like any real trouble.

JEFF. You get me a run-down on those Vigilantes. Trouble's where you least expect it.

SYD. *(with list)* The rest is all here. Saloons, cribs, dance halls, fancy ladies, gamblers, bunco men, strong arms... one big old mess of danger, just waiting for someone to put it all together.

BOWERS. In a word, wide open and welcoming as the arms of the Good Lord. Our move, Colonel Smith.

JEFF. Well done. Now listen up. Rules for Skagway. One: never hustle the residents, only passers-through.

Two: speak well of the town, Law and Order, God and Family, you know the hee-haw. Three: I am Colonel Smith. We never met before Skagway. There is no gang. There is no gang. There is no gang. *(All nod.)* What'd I just say, Red Gibbs?

RED. *(caught drinking BURKE's whiskey)* Wha...?

JEFF. Bad luck to drink from a dead man's glass.

RED. *(Grins, tosses back drink, sings.)*

DEAR LORD, YOU MADE WHISKEY AND WOMEN
OR SO BY ME MAM I WAS TOLD
WELL THANKS FOR THE WHISKEY
AND THE WOMEN AND ALL
BUT MOST OF ALL THANKS FOR THE BEAUTIFUL GOLD
GOLD...!
FOR THE BEAUTIFUL GOLD.

(a toast) Your health, Colonel Smith. Welcome to paradise!!! *(Tension breaks at last. With whoops, the gang welcomes its leader.)*

Scene Six

Gallows at the edge of town. Hanging dead by the neck, FRENCHIE VILLIERS. As scene unfolds, townspeople slowly gather on stage / in audience to gape. REVEREND DICKEY, PAUL McALEER and FRITZ come down aisle carrying coffin and shovel.

FRITZ.
'MORGEN MISTER DEAD MAN
WHAT DID YOU EAT FOR BREAKFAST?'
'I DIDN'T GET NO CHANCE TO EAT
THEY HUNG ME BY THE NECK, FIRST.'

'DEAD ON AN EMPTY STOMACH,
THAT'S A SORRY TALE YOU TELL
BUT DON'T YOU FEAR THERE'S PLENTY OF FOOD
AND DAMN WELL COOKED IN HELL, MAN.'
(As they near stage, FRITZ looks at audience.) Look at all dem people. Mackie. Tink dey never seen a dead man before, hey?

DICKEY. Thank you both for helping me. *(coughs)* I wish I could promise there won't be trouble.

FRITZ. Vigilantes, you mean? Hah! Dey can go trink dere own piss for vat I care. Dis little job here buys me a meal. Ven Fritz don't eat, Fritz ain't happy, right, Mackie?

DICKEY. You'll be paid as soon as I'm able, you have my word.

FRITZ. Vait a minute. Put down dat box, Mackie. I thought ve be paid on de job.

PAUL. He'll pay, Fritz, he promised.

FRITZ. I can't eat no promises. Two days mitout food...!

PAUL. We'll get credit against his word. No other worK around anyway.

FRITZ. Yah, yah, so Fritz vill do, but Fritz ain't happy.

DICKEY. *(prayer)* Dear Lord, have mercy upon this poor man's soul. And have mercy upon those who performed this deed. You alone know what was in their hearts. It's not for us to judge your works, only to find understanding and love as best we can. *(coughs)* Dear Lord, give me the strength to carry on your work in this place. Give me strength. Amen.

PAUL and FRITZ. Amen....

FRITZ. Lift him a little, Mackie. Get de veight off dat knot so I untie it.

(WHITMORE and BARKDULL have entered.)

WHIT. Taking him down already, Mr. Dickey?

DICKEY. He's been here for two days, Mr. Whitmore. I should think the point's been made.

WHIT. He was a murderer, that's what I'm told.

DICKEY. If so, he's certainly answered for it by now.

BARK. We think it's a good idea if he was left a little longer. Till the end of the week, say?

DICKEY. What *we* is that, Mr. Barkdull?

BARK. You just leave him where he is, Reverend...

WHIT. *(stopping him)* I have two jobs down at the dock just come open. Dollar-fifty an hour. You boys interested?

FRITZ. Ven do ve start?

WHIT. How 'bout right away?

DICKEY. They can finish here first, Mr. Whitmore.

WHIT. Jobs'll be gone if they wait. *(to crowd)* I need two lightermen down at the docks, no experience necessary, first come, first hired, dollar-fifty an hour.

ACT I THE BALLAD OF SOAPY SMITH

FRITZ. *(Stops crowd.)* Stay vere you are. Dem jobs is taken. Mackie, kommen sie...

PAUL. I'll stop by right after work, Reverend. He'll keep in this weather. I need the money. *(WHITMORE / BARKDULL exit with FRITZ and PAUL. DICKEY coughs, climbs onto coffin and tries to sever ropes over FRENCHIE's head with the shovel blade.)*

(Enter TAGISH SAM, a Tagish Indian in furs and bowler hat.)

SAM. Why Mr. Dickey no coat? Very cold. Bad-bad.

DICKEY. Sam, help me, please.

SAM. Him dead man.

DICKEY. I want to bring him up to Moore's Hill and bury him.

SAM. Him give you money put him in ground?

DICKEY. No, Sam, it's simply something that must be done. He wasn't a good man, they say, but he deserves a Christian burial.

SAM. *(hat out, upside down)* You put money, Sam help.

DICKEY. I'm afraid I have no money, Sam.

SAM. You have much money, Sam see. Sunday you talk good. You say God do this-and-that. People listen good. You take hat. People put money. Good business.

DICKEY. That wasn't for me, Sam. That was for my work here.

SAM. Sam work, too. No money, bad business. *(He dons hat, exits.)*

DICKEY. *(appeals)* Will somebody please help me, for

the love of God? I'll see that no harm comes to you. *(He collapses into long fit of coughing.)*

(Enter KITTY CHASE.)

KITTY. Uncle! They said I'd find you here. I thought you had some men helping you.
DICKEY. Go back to the sick tent, Kitty. This is no place for you to be.
KITTY. *(to crowd)* How can you all see what this poor man is trying to do and not lift a finger to help? What kind of people are you, anyway? Isn't there a single decent Christian among you?

(Gunshot. The body falls, rope severed above head by single bullet. Enter JEFF, revolver out, calmly placing one new bullet in chamber as he speaks. Crowd shrinks back, afraid.)

JEFF. Stay right where you are, folks. It's bad manners to walk away when a lady's addressing you. Go on, ma'am, that sounded right fascinating.
KITTY. Who are you?
JEFF. Beg pardon, Smith's the name, Colonel Smith, at your service, ma'am.
KITTY. Please put the gun away, Colonel. We don't need that.
JEFF. Yes, ma'm. Folks, the Reverend here needs assistance. I have five dollars apiece for the first two men who volunteer. *(Crowd pushes forward.)* My oh my, right heap o' Christians we have here all of a sudden. You ... and you.

MAN 1. Let's see the money.

JEFF. *(money out)* Reverend, these two fine Christian gentlemen are pleased to donate their day's wages towards your good works in the town... *(Two men start walking away.)*

JEFF. *(Pulls gun and aims.)* One more step, my friends, and there'll be two more holes to dig. With your permission, ma'm. Folks, I am in a regular fury of incomprehension about something here. It is my understanding that every one of you present knows who hung this man, is that right? Why do you look away? He was a criminal and he learned as all criminals must that crime does not pay. No, what baffles me is why the forces of law and order hereabouts are reduced to executing justice in such a furtive and clandestine manner. Why are we not ready to join hands with men of righteousness and shout from the rooftops, "I believe in Skagway, and I'll fight with you to make it a safe and decent place to live." My friends, I am going to show you something now and I want you to watch real careful, because this is a glimpse of the future of Skagway town. *(Mounts coffin and brandishes money.)* I have in my hand a United States Treasury Bill for the sum of five hundred dollars. You heard me. Not five, not fifty, but five whole centuries of folding green. Ever seen one of these up close before? Of course you haven't, there's only three of 'em in the entire world. Would you like to have a look? Then here's what you do. Just come on over to Jeff Smith's Oyster Parlor at the corner of 6th and Broadway, formerly Frank Clancy's Saloon, now under new management serving fine food and adult beverages round the clock, and there on the counter you will see this little miracle of American abundance on display in a glass jar marked CHURCH FUND. Anyone that adds ten dollars or more to that jar, drinks are on me for the rest of the day. Yes, my friends, we are going to build the Reverend here the finest House of God in all Territorial Alaska, because that's the way to show the world what we stand for here in Skagway: not a criminal hanging by the neck, but a tall white steeple, gleaming in the sunlight, proof positive to every passing steamer that the laws of God and man are with us in Skagway. What do you say???!!! *(Crowd cheers.)* Then come on over to Jeff Smith's. We're open for business as of RIGHT NOW!!! *(Crowd rushes off for a good time.)* Pardon the gun, ma'm. Reverend, I expect I'll be seeing more of you. *(He tips hat and exits. KITTY and DICKEY stare after him.)*

Scene Seven

PAUL McALEER, notebook in hand, specs on, comes forward and reads.

PAUL.
'TIS TRUE THEY CALLED IT HELL ON EARTH
ERE COLONEL SMITH APPEARED
YET IN WEEKS SKAGWAY GREW QUIETER
AND STRANGELY FREE FROM FEAR

HOW IT HAPPENED NONE COULD SAY
WILD RUMORS FLEW AROUND
BUT IN TRUTH 'TWAS LIKE AN UNSEEN HAND
WAS MOVING, MOVING THROUGH THE TOWN
UNSEEN THROUGHOUT THE TOWN.
(He closes notebook and addresses us.) I came north with one simple truth in my heart, a family teaching. It goes like this: You take out of the world only as much as you put into it, get less and there's an injustice, take more and there's a crime. But then one night, deep in the autumn of '97, stranded in Skagway, hungry and broke, I wrangled myself an innocent evening's employment with a certain Colonel Jefferson Randolph Smith. And it turned out to be the night that changed my life.

Scene Eight

JEFF SMITH's Oyster Parlor. Completely redecorated with potted palms, mirrors, elegant table service on white linen. Gala dinner just ending. Guests: FRANK REID & KITTY (together), STRONG, BARKDULL & WIFE, WHITMORE & WIFE, SHERPY & WIFE, other town notables (if possible). At head table, JEFF SMITH flanked by DICKEY and his WIFE. WILDER supervises FRANK CLANCY nad PAUL McALEER (as waiters). Each place setting has a bottle of whiskey in bright wrapping paper, some already open and in use. WHITMORE bangs knife on glass for silence.

WHIT. Quiet, everyone, quiet down. Now we've all spoke our two cents worth tonight, but before we go home I'd like to add a penny in the form of a toast. Tomorrow we break ground for a brand new church and infirmary, and we've all worked damn hard for it, pardon my Latin, Reverend. But there's one man here who deserves particular credit for getting the ball rolling, not to mention this fine hoop-de-doo he laid on for us tonight. His eating house is a welcome addition to the recreational facilities of Skagway. Here's to my good friend, Colonel Jefferson Randolph Smith. *(cheers)*

BARK. What about Frank Reid? He hasn't said his thanks yet. *(All encourage REID.)*

REID. *(Stands awkwardly.)* Colonel. Thanks for the meal. Food was tasty. I enjoyed myself. Oh, and the church ... and the infirmary. That was good of you. I guess if it's all as up and up as it looks like, well, none of us'll have anything to regret.

WHIT. *(dead silence)* I'd like to know just what the hell that's supposed to mean!

JEFF. *(diplomat)* It means Frank Reid is a man who smells his food before he eats it. May we all be as wise one day. *(a toast)* Frank, here's to you.

STRONG. Three cheers for Colonel Smith. Hip-hip... *(HOORAH!!!! etc. JEFF presents DICKEY with a model of the church stuffed full of banknotes and gold. Cheers. Guests begin to leave, JEFF bidding them farewell individually. First KITTY and REID.)*

JEFF. My. but don't the two of you look charming together. So nice of you to grace our festivities, Miss Chase.

KITTY. It was most educational, Colonel.

JEFF. Frank, didn't you get yourself a little thank-you bottle?

REID. You go ahead and drink that on me.

JEFF. Don't be a stranger, y'hear? *(REID /KITTY exit. Then comes the BARKDULLS and the WHITMORES.)* Calvin, Mrs. Barkdull, nice of you to attend. Mrs. Whitmore, what a fetching gown. *(to WHITMORE)* Oh, Bill, I had a word with Captain Reese. He agreed to put in at your docks exclusively from now on.

WHIT. You mean *The Excelsior*?

JEFF. And every other steamer in the line.

WHIT. By God, that's good, that's damn good.

JEFF. I'd say it's your docks that are good, Bill. Major Strong, I want to thank you for hiring those two boys. I think you'll find they make excellent sales clerks.

STRONG. Any time I can be of service, Colonel.

JEFF. I'll keep that very much in mind, Major. *(Exit WHITMORES and BARKDULLS and STRONG.)* Mrs. Sherpy, Mike, thanks for the excellent advice on the guest list. Impressive group, very well selected.

SHERPY. My pleasure, Jeff.

JEFF. And run my restaurant ad double size for a few weeks. Never mind the expense. A strong press is the backbone of a democracy, wouldn't you say?

SHERPY. I appreciate that. *(SHERPY and WIFE exit. MRS. DICKEY is holding two bottles of whiskey, her husband the church.)*

MRS. D. These will be for the infirmary, you understand.

JEFF. Well, I certainly hope so, ma'm.

DICKEY. I must tell you this is all rather peculiar for me, Colonel. It would seem that I owe my good fortune to a saloon.

JEFF. Please, Reverend, a restaurant.

DICKEY. Call it what you will.

JEFF. The good Lord works in mysterious ways.

DICKEY. To be sure. *(DICKEY and WIFE exit.)*

JEFF. *(Waves them good-bye, closes door, turns and whoops.)* Saints in heaven above, if bullshit floated we'd have to get us a whole new ceiling in here. Was this a beautiful evening or was it a beautiful evening.

WILD. It seemed to go pretty good.

JEFF. All those fine, upstanding burghers of Skagwaytown drifting home through the streets with their giftwrapped bottles of illegal whiskey, and the whole town whispering how Jeff Smith's in tight with the power. Damn, ain't a good hustle a stimulating thing. What do you say we celebrate. Clancy, pop on over to Mattie Silks and have her send us a couple sporting ladies, young and pretty.

CLANCY. Right you are, Jeff. *(exiting)*

WILD. And tell 'em to wash first. *(CLANCY is gone.)*

(BOWERS appears in door to rear room, deck of cards in hand.)

BOWERS. If the fat cats have all gone home, us skinny mice would like to commence our nightly game of cards. Shall we deal you gentlemen in?

WILD. In a minute, Charlie. *(BOWERS exits.)*

JEFF. *(sensing something's up)* Whiskey, old son? *(WILD-*

ER signals that PAUL is in the room. JEFF signals back that it's all right.)

WILD. You don't really think you got those people fooled, do you?

JEFF. Let's just say we took a big problem off their hands. Skagway's quieting down. They don't know the exact how and wherefore of it, but they smell the fact that my presence here has an improving effect upon the sporting population and they are very grateful, and I am very welcome in their town.

WILD. Then how come your face got all red and blotchy when they started making speeches. For a minute there I could've sworn you were swallowing all that bunco.

JEFF. Lighten up, old son, this is an evening of high horseshit and joy abounding.

WILD. You were moved, Jeff. For real. I know you, remember. You got a good act, but not that good.

JEFF. Oh, all right, so I was moved, George, so what? The emotion was purely aesthetical. I was flooded with feelings of brotherhood for all those present here tonight. Sure. All of us living off the passers-through. All of us seeking minimum means to maximum profit.

WILD. Cut the horseshit, Jeff. You never handled things like this before. We should be dealing with these people on the quiet. All this public display just draws unnecessary attention to our presence.

JEFF. Cultivation and planting, old son. The harvest comes hereafter.

WILD. Harvest? Jeff, this is a hit and run operation,

that was the plan, end of next summer latest, then back to the world.

JEFF. What world, George? We've worn our welcome a trifle thin most places south of Canada.

WILD. So that's it. You're planning to make this a long term set-up. No deal, Jeff. I bankrolled this operation and I say we don't work this shit-hole a day more than we have to, and if you don't like it, just hand me back my five-hundred dollars and I'll be gone.

JEFF. And what if come summer the Klondike strike proves genuine? Think, George. We might take root here. Prosper. Do very well for ourselves for a very long time.

WILD. Are you out of your mind? We're only running about a week ahead of our reputation as it is.

JEFF. Reputation??!! Georgie-boy, you show me a good reputation and I'll show you the grandson of a horse thief, but a horse thief who grabbed the power early on and played as dirty as he had to to keep it. Remember that tombstone in Jacksonville: ANY OLD FOOL CAN STRIKE IT RICH / THE GETTING WAS EASY / THE KEEPING A BITCH? You just hold on tight to that power and the day will come when your sons and your sons' sons'll be able to look any man in the eye and say 'my name is Smith, Jr., and I come from a long line of soldiers and statesmen,' and that man's brain'll be thinking 'bullshit' but his mouth'll be saying, 'Why, yes, Smith, Jr., I believe I did read of your illustrious lineage,' and that's cause his mouth is smart enough to know that Smith, Jr., inherited the power to put him in jail and run him out of town and make him bleed from the seams in all kinds of, by then, very legal and respectable ways. Power, George, that's all a good reputation is in the end: Bullshit with power behind it. *(to PAUL)* You finding all this pretty interesting, son?

PAUL. *(covering)* Beg pardon, sir?

JEFF. See, now there's a man with a smart mouth on him.

(Enter TAGISH SAM and TRIPOD SCHULTZ.)

TRI. Got a minute, Jeff?

JEFF. What you got for me, Tripod?

TRI. Red Onion Saloon won't pay up. Two gamblers in on the Ning Chow tonight, here's the names, they're staying over to the Burkhart Hotel, room 8. Fight over to the Grotto, ruffian name of Sloane, owner wants you to have a word with him. And this was in the evening mail pouch, outbound. *(He takes these things from a hollow with concealed door in his wooden leg, the only leg he has.)*

JEFF. *(Reads letter.)* "Editor, Seattle Post Intelligencer. I would appreciate information you might have about a man called Jefferson Randolph Smith who may style himself *Colonel*. Treat this as confidential. Awaiting your reply, I am yours ... Frank Reid, Town Engineer." *(pause)* Send this on, Tripod.

WILD. You can't let that go through. We were arrested in Seattle. It was in the papers.

JEFF. *(Gives TRIPOD money.)* Keep the change.

SAM. *(with money pouch)* All money collek tonight, good-good.

JEFF. Thank you, Sam. *(Gives tip. SAM and TRIPOD exit.)*

WILD. Not a very smart move, Jeff.

JEFF. Interesting man, Frank Reid. Held off this entire town without a gun, that's what they say. Yeah, first boatload of settlers went clawing over each other's back to grab the biggest piece of land for themselves and Frank Reid said, 'No, my friends, equal allotments, no favors, that's how this town begins,' and they backed off. Fascinating.

WILD. *(starting out)* I think I better have me a little talk with Mr. Reid.

JEFF. George, your little talks have an unfortunate habit of leading to premature self-defense.

WILD. Jeff, what the hell are you playing at?

JEFF. I'm the one that'll have a little talk with Mr. Reid.

WILD. We can't afford to lose another town.

JEFF. We won't. Your investment is safe.

WILD. I'm playing cards. *(He exits into back room.)*

JEFF. *(Lights cigar, watching PAUL who, nervous, drops tray.)* Waiting tables ain't your long suit, is it, son?

PAUL. This is my first time, actually.

JEFF. 'Actually?' My-oh-my, that's a pretty fancy usage ... actually. You educated or something?

PAUL. A little bit, I guess.

JEFF. Well what's a little-bit-I-guess educated young feller like yourself doing waiting tables in Skagway? You down on your luck?

PAUL. As a matter of fact, I did have a little setback.

JEFF. What happened? Go on, shoot.

PAUL. Well, I was headed for the gold fields and I had my pocket picked. Two-hundred-fifty dollars, every penny I owned. I was drinking with the man, I know what he looks like, but I can't seem to find him. Maybe you know something about him? Bud Peele he called himself. Baldish, 'bout yay high. Does that ring a bell?

JEFF. Whatever possessed you to think I'd know anything about a Bud Peele who picked your pocket?

PAUL. It's just you seem to know ... a lot of different kind of people around here ... that's all.

JEFF. I see. You have business in the gold fields?

PAUL. I just want to see 'em first hand. Get the feel, you know. Watch people coping in the wilds, maybe do a book of poems and sell 'em to a printer. It's a pretty popular subject right now.

JEFF. You're a poet!!! For a minute there I had you figured for a man with his head nailed on right.

PAUL. It's no worse an ambition than yours ... than many.

JEFF. And what is my ambition?

PAUL. I don't know, sir.

JEFF. That's right, son. You've heard some talk tonight, but never judge a man by what he says, son, watch what he does, just watch what he does. Things are rarely what they seem to be.

PAUL. Yes, sir.

JEFF. Take me, for instance. Now to look at, you'd not think I was a lover of poetry, whereas, in truth, quality verse is my passion.

PAUL. No, sir, I sure wouldn't have guessed that.

JEFF.
WHILST KINGS AND WARRIORS CLANG ABOUT
THIS MOILING EARTH ON FEARSOME STEED
AND CONQUERED NATIONS TO THEIR FEET
DO GOLDEN TREASURES BRING
YET ALONE OF ALL THIS STRIFE AND NOISE
SHALL BE REMEMBERED THOSE FEW DEEDS
THE MUSE, IN SILENT ECSTASY, DID MOVE
SOME LONELY POET TO SING.

PAUL. That's wonderful. Keats? *Wordsworth!*

JEFF. Smith, *Soapy.* Old trick I learned from Billy DeVere, the Tramp Poet. Just let your mind go blank, talk elevaterd and rhyme it up every now and then, that's poetry. Billy charged two dollars a verse, what do you get?

PAUL. I don't know. I never sold a poem ... yet.

JEFF. Well now are you or are you not a poet? Think careful before you answer, because I deal with a man as he calls himself.

PAUL. I haven't written a whole lot. My friends say I'm pretty good at it. It's what I want to do. I don't know what to say. Yeah, I'm a poet.

JEFF. *(chuckles)* Hard to know for sure without a little confirmation from outside, ain't it? All right, son, if a poet's what you want to be, then that's what you'll be for me. And you better not let me down. Ever.

PAUL. You want me to write you a poem?

JEFF. There ya go. Something on the grand scale. Like *The Anead*, ever hear of that one?

PAUL. Of course.

JEFF. All about the founding of a town. Good subject,

don't you think? Skagway, for instance. Start with a deserted meadow on the Lynn Canal, virgin land, primeval, God's country. Suddenly, rumors of gold six hundred miles inland, and a narrow pass discovered through the mountains leading right down here to the shore. Boom, overnight a town is born. Muddy streets, wooden shacks, tents, hungry dogs roaming around, you know, get in some local color. Enter... a stranger... a man of mystery. He's looking for a place to put his life in ord.... never mind. Just tell how he tames the town, brings law and order out of chaos. Religion. Government. Prosperity. Whatever. Put in a few gunfights, and don't eschew sentiment, folks eat it up. Yeah, that sounds pretty good, what do you think?

PAUL. I think you must be joking with me.

JEFF. Poetry is excellent propaganda. I'll tell you what... *(money out)* ... here's two hundred fifty to start. And upon satisfactory completion I'll give you seven hundred fifty more, plus my permission to leave town.

PAUL. Pardon?

JEFF. Now, son, you could have left the room when George and I got to talking. You thought about it. I watched you. But curiosity got the better of you. Look me in the eye, son. If you stay, you play. Otherwise, you know enough to be one hell of a problem for me.

PAUL. Yes, sir.

(enter two prostitutes)

PRO 1. We're from Mattie Silks. Are you our friendly boys?

JEFF. *I* am, darling. Oh, Mr. Poet, maybe you'd like to take your ease? What's your pleasure, Tweedle-dum or Tweedle-dee?

PAUL. I have to finish up in here.

JEFF. You're excused for the night, while I still have some dishes left.

PAUL. In that case, maybe I'd better start writing.

JEFF. Never refuse a gift from your benefactor. *(to PRO 2)* You treat him real nice, darling, and maybe one day he'll immortalize you in verse.

PRO 2. Oh...!

(enter DOC from back room)

DOC. Your seat is open, Colonel.

JEFF. Oh, Doc, our newest associate is looking for a pickpocket name of Bud Peele. Are you familiar with any such man?

DOC. Bud Peele? I believe so. *(With a fluid gesture, he takes off his thick glasses and removes a hat and wig, revealing Mr. Peele.)*

PAUL. You!!! Where's my two hundred fifty dollars?

JEFF. It's right there in your hand, son. See that, ain't nothing what it seems to be, and you owe me a poem. Welcome aboard, Mr. Poet!!! *(blackout)*

END OF ACT ONE

ACT TWO
Scene One

The new church. Unfinished raw wood pews and alter. Behind curtained alcove to one side, the infirmary, nurses table in view. Two carpenters are at work. Enter from outside, KITTY, SYD DIXON and RED GIBBS, the two men supporting between them a limp and feverish patient in pyjamas clutching backpack to chest.

KITTY. Put him in bed and cover him well, he's been badly exposed. *(SYD and RED take the patient, JENSEN, into the infirmary as KITTY speaks quietly to the carpenters, who exit at her request.)*

JENS. *(Swedish accent)* I must go dere... Klondike... pass ban freeze up I don't go now ... I lose my claim ... I lose everything ... please, I go....

KITTY. *(getting thermometer)* You have cholera, Mr. Jensen. Thank your lucky stars these men found you in the snow. *(entering infirmary)* Put this under your tongue and lie back, there we are. *(She comes out to nurse's table followed by SYD.)*

SYD. Ma'm, any chance of a tad more pain-killer for my friend Mr. Clyde? His war wound is acting up something livid.

KITTY. You want more opium, Mr. Dixon?

47

SYD. Is *that* what it was? Well, it by God did the trick. My friend Mr. Clyde was feeling some better for that medication.

KITTY. I think ten grams is enough for one week, don't you, Mr. Dixon? Persuade your friend Mr. Clyde to forebear until Monday.

(RED has come up behind SYD, showing him a wallet in his belt.)

RED. Come on, Syd, we can go now. *(SYD follows RED out of the church.)*

(KITTY enters the infirmary as FRANK REID enters the church, clomps snow off boots and removes heavy overcoat. He is dressed well. KITTY re-enters church and goes to nurse's table.)

REID. Kitty....

KITTY. *(Sees him.)* Why, Mr. Reid, don't we look elegant today. What's the occasion?

REID. Just passing by. Thought I'd poke my nose in, see how you're getting along.

KITTY. We're chaotic but coping. If you can wait until my uncle returns, I'll steal a moment and give you the Cook's Tour.

REID. Fact is, I'd like to talk to you. It's a private sort of thing.

KITTY. I'm afraid I can't leave the infirmary unattended. Will this do? *(the church)*

REID. I've tried to catch your attention these past

couple Sundays. You always seem to end up on the other side of the room.

KITTY. Mr. Reid, why don't you tell me what this is all about.

REID. *(pause, awkward)* See, I've knocked around these Territories for a while now. Never found a place I thought to settle. Or someone to settle with. I got a few years on you, true enough, but I come from sturdy people, they live a long time, most of 'em. I'm regular in my habits. I don't use the tobacco. I take a drink every now and then, but I'm not intemperate. And I won't tolerate bad language, not in my own home, leastwise. *(pause)* I feel like I got three tongues in my mouth.

KITTY. Mr. Reid, are you proposing marriage?

REID. It's not coming out like I planned...

KITTY. Please, Mr. Reid, before you go any further ... I'm afraid I can't possibly accept.

REID. Maybe you'd like a little time to think it over.

KITTY. It's nothing to do with you, Mr. Reid, please believe that. You're a very fine and honorable man, and if you've decided to marry and live your life here, I'm sure you'll have no trouble making a suitable match.

REID. I like you very well, you know.

KITTY. And I feel very warmly towards you, Mr. Reid.

(enter REVEREND DICKEY with JEFF SMITH, in the midst of showing him around)

DICKEY. Ah, Mr. Reid, Kitty, dear, I was just showing our benefactor what he hath wrought. The workmen say they'll be finished Friday, so God willing we'll hold our first service Sunday week. After all you've done, I do hope you'll attend.

JEFF. I wouldn't miss it had I nine of my ten toes in the grave.

DICKEY. The church connects directly with the infirmary here so I can be called at all hours in case of emergency. My own idea, though I oughtn't to boast, vanity, vanity, oh dear me.... Mr. Reid, will you join us for tea?

REID. Some other time, Reverend. Thank you.

JEFF. Frank, can you spare a minute. I'll be right along, Reverend.

DICKEY. Yes, yes, I'll have my wife put the kettle on, and do forgive my chattering away like this, I'm so happy I don't know what to do with myself. Thank God for men like you, Colonel, thank God. *(exits)*

KITTY. Shall we thank God for you, Colonel?

JEFF. I wouldn't go so far, ma'm.

KITTY. Well, you've made my uncle very happy. I'm pleased that you see fit to include good works among your many fascinating activities in Skagway. Excuse me. *(She goes into the infirmary.)*

JEFF. *(Looks at REID, takes in the room. Pause.)* Odd to stand in a church again after all these years. I studied for the ministry, you know. It's true. There were those who considered me exceptionally promising. Of course that's neither here nor there, is it, now that you know the truth about me.

REID. What truth is that?

JEFF. No need to make light at my expense. What I left

at your office this morning was a declaration of good faith.

REID. No offense intended. I haven't been to my office yet.

JEFF. I see. Bad timing, then. Unusual for me. All right, you'll know when you get there anyway, so cards on the table. Does the name Soapy Smith mean anything to you?

REID. Wasn't there a confidence man went by that name? Had something of a reputation down the Territories a few years back. Sure, that rings a bell, why do you ask?

JEFF. Why do you think I ask?

REID. Man usually puts a question because he wants to know the answer.

JEFF. *(pause)* I'm Soapy Smith. That's right, you're looking at the man himself.

REID. I'll be darned. You know, I had half a hunch there might be some connection, what with that last name and all. So, you're Soapy Smith.

JEFF. I am. And I am not. Oh, to look at it's the same old outfit you heard tell of, but inside where you can't see, there's a very different man. A man who's realised he's running out of places to set up. Yes, circumstances have forced me to take a good hard look at what I've made of my life. Frightening to see yourself with no more illusions, no more excuses. Sin and redemption. That's what they taught us in the ministry. Sin and redemption. You see, Frank, when I come up here I found myself making a little pact with the Good Lord. Show me the way, dear Lord, show me the way to redeem myself and I swear I shall use those precious gifts you gave me and that I've squandered all these years, I shall use them to win back your blessing for ever and ever, amen. That was my vow.

REID. Isn't this a little irregular, Jeff? You're telling me things that friends say to each other, but you and me, we're barely acquainted.

JEFF. You may turn out to be the only friend I have in this town.

REID. I thought you had all kinds of interesting friends around here.

JEFF. You mean the habitues of my so-called saloon? Men who'd sell your life for a dime and never lose a wink of sleep dreaming on it.

REID. A man chooses the company he keeps.

JEFF. And by them is he known, is that it? Tell me, Frank, what if that company is the kind who hang a man by night, hang him hideously and without due process of law? Are you to be known by the company *you* keep?

REID. Jeff, if you got something in mind, you better get to it. I have a lot of work to do.

JEFF. Very well. From where I sit, I can penetrate into every dark corner of this town, learn it inside and out in a way no lawman could ever do. Now then, armed with that information, what if I wanted the same thing for Skagway as you do?

REID. Jeff, what exactly is it you're asking me for?

JEFF. *(pause)* Time, Frank. Time. Don't judge or move against me until the spring. I know how to put things right in this town, *entirely* right, and that's what I aim to do, but in my own way, because it's the only way there is.

You see, our means differ, but our ends are the same.

REID. I doubt that, Jeff. I very much doubt that.

JEFF. Then you be the judge. I'm placing in your hands the power to destroy me.

REID. What power?

JEFF. The complete truth. Newspaper clippings of all my past exploits. I left them in an envelope in your office. If by spring I prove less than what I say, just hand the town that envelope and I'm a dead man in Skagway.

REID. Newspaper clippings? *(slow smile)* So that's what this is all about. You intercepted my letter, didn't you? Hadn't figured you got men in the post office yet. You're a fast worker.

JEFF. *(pause)* I check real careful when my life is on the line.

REID. You misunderstand, Jeff. I'm not out to get you. What you did in the past is your own business. I just like to know the facts of a situation is all. As for those clippings, well, if you're half as slick as I figure, you knew that information would come out in time and you got yourself well covered.

JEFF. I find it just a little bit ironic that when I tell the truth at last, the man I've carefully selected to trust doesn't seem to believe a word I've said. Now why is that, Frank, why don't you trust me?

REID. I don't know, Jeff. That's the truth. I like you well enough. I do. I guess it's just something about you that makes me smile. *(Starts out.)*

JEFF. I am not an entertainer, Frank Reid.

REID. I'll drop by later and return your press clippings. *(REID exits. JEFF watches him go, then exits into*

DICKEY's quarters at rear of church. PAUL McALEER enters, dressed in new and fashionable suit. He looks towards the infirmary.

PAUL. Miss Chase ... I need some medicine ... for my throat.

(KITTY comes into church.)

KITTY. Mackie, I told you never to meet me here. You promised.

PAUL. I have something for you.

KITTY. Not now, I'll see you Wednesday ... your clothes!

PAUL. I was wondering when you'd notice. Hand tailored. From Capelli, that Eye-talian deal over on 7th.

KITTY. I thought you didn't have any money.

PAUL. *(pause)* And this is for you. *(ring box)* Go on, open it. It'll only take a minute, then I'll go, I promise.

KITTY. If you ever come here again, I swear it's the last time you'll see me. Do you understand? *(PAUL nods. She opens box.)*

PAUL. It's a gold heart. Fourteen karats. Made in Paris ... France. And that's a poem for you. Go on, read it.

KITTY.
LOVE, A THOUSAND SWEET DISTILLINGS
AND WITH NECTAR BOSOMS FILLING
CHARM ALL EYES THAT NONE MAY FIND US
BE ABOVE, BEFORE, BEHIND US
AND WHILE WE THY PLEASURES TASTE
ENFORCE TIME TO STAY

AND BY THE FORELOCK HOLD HIM FAST
LEST OCCASION SLIP AWAY.
You wrote this for me?

PAUL. Do you like it?

KITTY. Take it back.

PAUL. What's wrong?

KITTY. Give it to me Wednesday. I'll pretend I never saw it. And we'll meet in the usual place, and you'll give me the heart ... no, first you'll read me the poem, then you'll give me the heart and then ... I will thank you properly.

PAUL. Properly?

KITTY. Go, Mackie.

PAUL. Does that mean you've decided?

KITTY. Wednesday.

PAUL. But *what,* Wednesday? You'll decide, or you've already decided and Wednesday you'll let me...

KITTY. I've decided that if you leave right now and promise never to meet me here during the day, it is very possible that Wednesday I'll allow you ... to kiss me, now go, Mackie.

PAUL. *(pause)* If you've already made up your mind, why wait until Wednesday?

KITTY. One more word and I may change my mind.

PAUL. I'm going to kiss you, Kitty Chase.... *(advances)*

KITTY. You'll do no such thing. Stop it, Mackie, are you mad, this is an infirmary.

PAUL. I don't care. I'll kiss you right out in front of all the sick people. Show 'em something worth getting better for.

KITTY. *(retreating)* If you dare....

PAUL. What'll happen if I dare...?

KITTY. Don't, Mackie, don't come any closer ... please... *(PAUL kisses KITTY. Shocked at first, she slowly yields to new feelings.)*

(From behind the infirmary curtain we hear JENSEN's voice.)

JENS. MY VALLET!!! VAR MY VALLET IS GONE? VAS HERE INSIDE MY PACK.

KITTY. *(Breaks kiss.)* Go, Mackie!!!

PAUL. *(exiting)* Wednesday....

(JENSEN stumbles into church clutching his pack.)

JENS. I ban robbed. Dem two men, dey take avay my vallet. All my monies she ban in dere...

KITTY. Mr. Jensen, you're delerious. Now lie down and be quiet while I give you something to help you sleep.

JENS. I BAN ROB-BED. I BAN ROB-BED. I BAN ROB-BED.

Scene Two

PAUL McALEER comes forward, addresses us.

PAUL. I'll tell you, before that day, I never knew what

a little spending money could do for a man's self confidence. Miss Katherine Halliwell Chase, a lady from straight out of the fashion plates, Baltimore educated, quality folk, and there I was coming right out and kissing her. On the lips. You saw. So in case you were wondering if I minded being stuck in Skagway that winter ... not at all, my friends, not at all. Oh, small confession. That poem. You notice how I never come right out and said I wrote it. That's cause I didn't. It's by James Shirley, a minor Elizabethan I was hoping they'd overlooked in her eastern education. All's fair in love. I guess you could say I was picking up a trick or two myself, working for the Colonel. *(Strikes stance, reads from notebook.)*
JEFF'S SECRET SOUL THROUGH DARKEST NIGHT
SLEPT ON WITH RESTLESS DREAMS
IMMACULATE AND INNOCENT
OF WHAT FATE HAD DECREED

THEN CAME THE NIGHT THAT DESTINY
DID WAKE HIS SOUL FROM SLEEP
AND CALL IT FORTH INTO THE WORLD
FOR ALL MANKIND TO MEET
HIS SOUL FOR ALL MANKIND TO MEET

Scene Three

MATTIE SILK's dance hall. Riotous night in full swing. Miners dance and carouse. Dance hall girls serve drinks, flirt, dance, etc. Band finishes a riproaring tune and MATTIE leaps onto the stage.

MATTIE. Evening, friends.

ALL. Evening, Mattie.

MATTIE. More drinks over there, girls, look alive. Ladies and gentlemen, and anything else that might've wandered in... Winter is upon us, cold and cruel, the passes are frozen shut, and here you are, tomorrow's millionaires, stuck in Skagway alone and unloved. All but *one* of you, that is. *(cheers)* That's right, you roosters, it's the moment you've all been waiting for, the Saturday Night Bonanza Winter Raffle, and here to tell you all about it is our very own and darling Colonel Jefferson Randolph Smith.

JEFF. *(Mounts stage to cheering.)* Professor... *(Piano plays sadly.)* My friends, last week a poor young creature came to Mattie Silks destitute and said, "Mattie, my onliest sister just died in San Francisco leaving three homeless babes. I want to send for them in the poorhouse but the price of three steamer tickets is beyond my means, help me, oh help me please." Well, that's just what we're gonna do. Every penny of tonight's raffle is going to that young lady, and in return, she will offer herself in gratitude as a winter wife to the man with the winning ticket. It is my privilege and my pleasure to introduce to you the chaste, the virginal, the lovely Miss Margaret McNally!!!

(Enter MOLLIE FEWCLOTHES, a prostitute dressed as a virgin bride. Crowd hoots.)

MINER 1. That ain't no virgin, that's Mollie Fewclothes, she's a whoo-er.

ACT II THE BALLAD OF SOAPY SMITH 59

MINER 2. I caught a dose off her last month...

MOLLIE. And yer the bastard run off 'thout payin, too.

JEFF. Silence, Philistines, there is a maiden in our midst. Now then, raffle tickets are fifty dollars apiece, vendors will pass among you while Miss McNally displays her vocal endowments in a song penned special by Skagway's own poet laureate, Paul McAleer. *(PAUL rises to cheers.)* Professor.

MOLLIE. *(Piano plays. She sings.)*
A VIRGIN PRINCESS FROM VIRGINEE
DID MARRY A KLONDIKER KING
SHE TAUGHT HIM TO EAT WITH A KNIFE AND A FORK
HE BOUGHT HER A BIG DIAMOND RING

THEN HE BUILT HER A SWEET LITTLE CASTLE
THE SERVANTS THEY CAME WHEN SHE RANG
YOU NEVER DID SEE A MORE HAPPIER COUPLE
AND THIS IS THE SONG THAT SHE SANG

A MAN FROM ALASKA DID WIN ME
FOR LOVE I WENT DOWN ON ME KNEE
I THREW BOTH MY ARMS ROUND HIS GOLD-MINER'S BODY
AND DID WHAT HE ASKED ME
AND DID IT FOR FREE...

(Wild cheers. During this, several militiamen have entered, armed and in uniform. The place goes quiet.)

MILITIAMAN. Who is the proprietor of this establishment?

MATTIE. I am she.

JEFF. What's your problem, son? *(The head militiaman, CORPORAL EGAN, takes a handbill from under his arm and reads it out.)*

EGAN. "Be it known: The public serving of spiritous beverages in the proximity of designated indian populations being an inducement to fits of ungovernable violence and licentiousness, is hereby declared illegal. By order of the District Commissioner of Southwest Territorial Alaska, all premises serving said beverages are in violation of the law and therefore closed and off limits this day of January 28th, 1898." It's after two, folks, you have five minutes to clear the premises. *(to MATTIE)* Post this on your door and remain closed until further notice. *(Miners begin to leave, reluctantly, pushed by militia.)* All right, folks, let's get a move on. You have five minutes to clear out or we will haul you in.

JEFF. Corporal, may I ask where these orders of yours originate?

EGAN. Commissioner Sehlbrede. He's at City Hall if you have any questions.

JEFF. Who the hell is Commissioner Sehlbrede?

EGAN. Posted in Dyea yesterday, sir. He's the new man.

JEFF. Corporal, my name is Jefferson Smith... Colonel Jefferson Smith, Texas Border Cavalry, Seventh Territorial Regulars. I am also Chairman of the Law and Order Committee of Skagway, and I don't recall sending for you...

EGAN. You wouldn't happen to be the one they call "Soapy" Smith, would you?

JEFF. I am *Colonel* Jefferson Randolph Smith and I am your superior officer. I will overlook your insolence, soldier, but I will not tolerate insubordination. You just trot your men back on over to Dyea on the double, that's an order, Corporal.

EGAN. Why don't you take that up with the Commissioner, *Mister* Smith. *(turns)* All right, men, next saloon's around the corner, let's move with a purpose.

JEFF. Don't you turn your back on me you officious son of a bitch. I'll have those stripes ripped clean off your arm. Nobody talks to me like that. Nobody!!! *(Militia is gone. Room empty but for JEFF, WILDER, MATTIE and PAUL McALEER.)*

WILD. Take it easy, Jeff, those boys are real military.

JEFF. And I am a real Colonel, god damn it. In this town I am what I *say* I am. Who the hell is this Sehlbrede outfit, anyway? How could there be a new man here and I don't know a thing about it? This is not good, George, this is not good.

WILD. There's only about fifteen soldiers in the entire district. Even if they're all in Skagway tonight, our boys outnumber 'em five to one. Why not just arm up, head over to City Hall and eradicate the problem? That's how we did it in Denver.

JEFF. That's why we're living in Skagway. I do not aim to conquer this town by force. I will win it over heart and soul and insure my unqualified welcome.

WILD. What happened to all that stuff about bullshit

with power behind it?

JEFF. I'm re-adjusting my outlook, George. It's a sign of personal growth.

WILD. This whole town's just been closed down, Jeff. Do you understand that? If we don't do something and quick, we've lost the ranch.

JEFF. *(pacing, stops)* Wait a minute. What if, instead of a gang of thugs, *we* were an army. I mean official, commissioned by the President of the United States. Uniforms, red, white and blue, God and Country, the entire hee-haw, hell, everyone loves a patriot. We could stand tall and keep the militia out of here forever. After all, Washington's bound to see the pressing need to protect our shores up here.

WILD. From what?

JEFF. The enemy, George, the enemy.

WILD. What enemy?

JEFF. Well.... Spain? Sure, didn't I read they attacked our battleship "The Maine" off Cuba? Who's to say Skagway's not next. Very ambitious nation, Spain. Mr. Poet, take this down... "Recruiting drive, goal, fifty men, hell, make it two hundred, we'll mix some regular folks in there, too. Secure valid military commission....."

WILD. *(He grabs notebook from PAUL, points at JEFF, trembling, odd.)* See my finger? It's pointing at you. A straight line. That's how you move from one place to another, straight lines. We're here for the money, period. That's a straight line. But you're moving all crooked. Sucking up to the nabobs. Strutting around like some god damn town dignitary. And now all this horseshit about a private army... commission from the president??!! What's going on, Jeff, cause I'm starting to wonder if you got a screw loose somewhere.

JEFF. *(steely)* I'm doing business same as always, George. How I go about that is my own affair. My intentions are a loaded gun, and you are standing with your back to me. Now do I have your trust, friend George?

WILD. *(pause)* I don't want to see anything bad happen to you, that's all. In this business it ain't easy to find new friends.

JEFF. You're a good old boy, George. The best in the world. *(He holds out hand. They shake.)*

(Enter CORPORAL EGAN with SEHLBREDE and REID.)

JEFF. Why, Frank, what an unexpected pleasure. I'd offer you refreshments, but we've just been closed down by the armies of God.

SEHL. *(Circles JEFF in silence. Stops.)* So, you're Soapy Smith, eh? Don't look like much to me.

REID. Jeff, this is Charles Sehlbrede, the new Commissioner. He wanted to meet you.

JEFF. The pleasure is all his, I'm sure.

SEHL. I have no desire to know you, Smith. Just understand one thing. My predecessor was pliable. I am not. I play by the book and I am a son of a bitch about the law.

JEFF. Now why start off on the wrong foot when there's so much we could do for each other? Let's just sit down together and talk things over.

SEHL. You think you're clever, Smith? That's good. I want you to keep thinking that. Because I'm waiting, and one day you'll be so clever you'll put a foot wrong, just once you'll take one tiny step off the straight and narrow, and on that day I'll swoop down from a great height and cause you severe damage.

JEFF. I run a nice little restaurant over at 6th and Broadway. Don't know of any law against that, do you?

SEHL. *(Exiting)* Mr. Reid.

JEFF. You disappoint me, Frank. I was hoping we'd become friends.

REID. Nothing personal, Jeff. It's just your associates are getting some funny ideas about what's acceptable in this town. Crooked gaming, protection rackets, extortion. I just want folks to see we got a new man who's not afraid to do his job. I want your associates to see that as well.

JEFF. What's the matter with you Vigilante boys? Don't you see you're gonna kill this town stone dead if you close down the good time action?

REID. It's only for one night. The militia returns to Dyea tomorrow.

JEFF. One night??!! You went and had this entire town put under martial law for one stinking night? I thought you Vigilantes wanted a good reputation for Skagway? This'll make us the laughing stock of Alaska.

REID. It wasn't the Vigilantes that called in Sehlbrede.

JEFF. Jesus God in Heaven, are you telling me you went and acted on your own? Do your hang-em-high friends know about this?

REID. I expect they'll find out pretty soon.

JEFF. Tell me, Frank, is there anything special you'd like engraved on your headstone?

REID. You've been looking at life crooked for too long, Jeff. Don't under-estimate the Vigilantes. *(Starts out.)*

JEFF. If you're so sure of 'em, how come you acted on your own?

REID. *(pause)* Night, Jeff. *(exits)*

WILD. Looks like your little talk with Frank Reid did us a whole pile of good.

JEFF. My God ain't he a clever man? In and out in one night and the whole town knows there's law nearby that'll come when they whistle. All right, Mr. Reid, if army's what you want to play, army's what we'll play. *(WILDER is up.)* Where you goin', George?

WILD. You play army, I'll go play with Mr. Reid.

JEFF. Sit down, George. One dead Frank Reid is no use to us at all. But Frank Reid alive, and in our pocket, now that could be a very valuable asset. How does it go, easiest to rope a steer that wanders from the herd...?

WILD. Frank Reid will never be in our pocket. We've seen his kind before.

JEFF. No, never his exact kind. Can't be bought. Can't be scared. Can't be fooled. The man is goodness itself. I want him. I'll have him.

WILD. Why, for God sake? He has nothing to offer us, nothing but trouble.

JEFF. Georgie-boy, you sound as if you're afraid of Mr. Reid.

WILD. I ain't afraid of anything a bullet can stop.

JEFF. Then put your money where your mouth is. How about we wager the big one? Your entire investment times two. Ten thousand dollars says by springtime I'll get Mr. Reid to shake my hand and say, "Jeff Smith, I had you all wrong, you're a fine fellow and I'm proud to call you friend."

WILD. I'm not playing any more games with you, Jeff.

JEFF. That's right, old son. From here on in it's all or nothing. *(handshake)* God damn, ain't nothing like high stakes to get the blood circulating. Yes, indeed, the pieces are all falling into place. It's harvest time! Mattie, Mr. Poet, get a good night's sleep. Tomorrow, bright and early, we're in the recruiting business. *(Exits, whistling patriotic tune.)*

WILD. *(pause)* Mattie, you got kerosene out back, don't you?

MATTIE. *(wary)* I might.

WILD. You know where Frank Reid's house is?

MATTIE. I might.

WILD. Some of the boys'll be over in a while. Point 'em in the right direction.

MATTIE. Didn't you ought to clear that with Jeff?

WILD. My partner's gone a little funny on the subject of Frank Reid, wouldn't you say?

MATTIE. That's his business.

WILD. And this is mine. Jeff's imagination plays tricks on him sometimes. And I don't like Frank Reid. Not at all. Just do like I say. *(exits)*

PAUL. *(pause)* Shouldn't we tell Jeff?

MATTIE. You stick to poetry, Mackie. Leave real life to the grown-ups. *(They click whiskey glasses.)*

Scene Four

A street. FRANK REID walking home. Out of the shadows step WHITMORE, BARKDULL, STRONG and SHERPY.

WHIT. You got some explaining to do, Frank Reid.

BARK. Why'd you call in the militia?

REID. *(pause)* Just thought folks ought to see we got law here for a change.

STRONG. God damn it, Frank, you can't do that. Get the law in here and they'll drown us all in a flood of lethal rules and regulations.

REID. Why don't you fellers come to my office tomorrow and we'll talk this whole thing over with Commissioner Sehlbrede?

WHIT. You don't have an office anymore. You've been relieved of your job and voted out of the Vigilantes. Act without us, you act against us, that's the rule.

REID. What the hell's going on here? I thought we all wanted Law and Order in this town.

WHIT. We want the sporting boys, is that plain enough for you? *Our* business needs *their* business.

BARK. Look around you, Frank. The streets are empty. The town is dead. That's how it'll be for good if the government gets ahold of this place.

STRONG. The law doesn't understand how we work around here, Frank.

REID. What doesn't it understand? You mean the ten percent you all pay Jeff to have his dock rats steer trade your way and run the competition out of town, cause I don't understand that, either. I thought Jeff was leaning on you to do business that way and you'd welcome the law to ease things, but my God, you actually seem to relish the stink we're living in. It's pathetic.

WHIT. You're a dangerous man, Frank Reid. You're arrogant and self-righteous and disloyal. If you make one more move against our interests....

REID. What, Bill? Do I join Frenchie Villiers on your list of noble deeds?

WHIT. You're such a good person, Frank. I know there's a place for you in heaven, and I'd think of it as doing God's work to speed you on your way.

REID. Good night, gentlemen. *(He starts to go. WHITMORE blocks him.)*

SHERPY. Frank, we need your word that from now on you'll keep your nose out of all activities effecting the law and commerce of the town. On that condition we'll allow you to stay here. Do you agree?

REID. Skagway is my home, gentlemen. It's my home.

BARK. And it's ours, too. So lay off. Because next time there won't be any warning.

WHIT. You'll just wake up dead in a little wooden box on Moore's Hill. *(WHITMORE and BARKDULL exit.)*

SHERPY. I'm sorry it has to be this way, Frank. *(He leaves.)*

STRONG. *(He lingers.)* Don't ignore the warning, Frank. I've always tried to stand by you, but I can't hold them back after what you did tonight.

REID. How come you're not looking at me, Jim? I hope to hell it's got something to do with shame.

STRONG. Just stop getting so God almighty upright on me. Because, remember, I saw you kill that man back in Oregon. It was self defense, sure. And that's what I mean. You did what you had to do. Well, so do I. If you want to go and atone for it until kingdom come, fine, but don't punish everyone around you with the same hard rules, because the world won't stand up to that kind of judgement. We bend, or we break. *(He leaves. FRANK REID stands alone.)*

Scene Five

Back room, JEFF SMITH's Oyster Parlor. PAUL at roll top desk doing paperwork. MATTIE sits half-asleep on chaise-lounge, champagne glass in hand. A lively melody playing on the Victrola. JEFF paces.

JEFF. *(calls)* TRIPOD!!!

(TRIPOD sticks head in door.)

JEFF. Any sign of George Wilder?
TRI. I'll tell you when he's coming, take it easy.
JEFF. Bring us some more champagne. *(exit TRIPOD)* Drink up, Mattie, Mr. Poet, drink to this night full of mischief. *(Record ends. He goes to wind it up.)*

MATTIE. I've never seen you like this, Jeff. You're jumpy as a cat.

JEFF. *(Leaves Victrola.)* My entire house of cards would've come tumbling down in this town tonight if you hadn't warned me of Mr. Wilder's incendiary plans.

PAUL. *(with champagne)* Have some of this, Jeff. It'll calm your nerves.

JEFF. Liquor and women, two things that'll mess your brains up. This will pass. It'll pass. *(paces)* Whole damn operation's growing like a weed out of control. The boys writing their friends back home, "Come to Skagway, it's carnival time." A list, for God's sake, I have to keep a list nowadays just to know who's working for me, and that ain't good, no sir, if it's out of your head it's out of your hands. *(yells)* TRIPOD, WHERE'S THAT CHAMPAGNE? What's he doing, sleeping on his crutches out there? Look at it, no discipline, no obedience. My own best friend, Mattie, how could he go and set an example like that?

MATTIE. Forget it, Jeff, no harm done.

JEFF. No harm, when he just went and damn near ruined my only chance.... *(stops)*

MATTIE. What chance?

JEFF. *(pause)* Oh, Mattie, if I am truely no more than what I've been till now, it was a sorry little journey indeed.

MATTIE. I don't think I want to know what you mean. You're just fine by me.

JEFF. *(chuckles)* You're an all-right woman, you know that? By God, if I was a little older, or you were a little younger, I'd probably go and do something stupid and marry you.

MATTIE. Who says I'd have you? Better men have tried.

JEFF. Who tried? You been married?

MATTIE. Hell, yes, dozens of times. In my own manner. For a night or two. That's the best of a man. After that it's all sore tempers and dirty laundry.

(Enter gang minus WILDER. BOWERS carries a kerosene can.)

BOWERS. Mission accomplished. It's a veritable flaming inferno.

JEFF. Mattie, shake the girls out of bed. It's a night full of mischief and we're gonna kick up dust till the devil goes to bed. *(MATTIE exits rear door. JEFF goes to crank up the Victrola.)*

(Enter WILDER from restaurant, distraught.)

JEFF. Why, George, perfect timing, the party just began.

WILD. Can I have a word with you? In private?

JEFF. In private? Wouldn't that make the boys think we had secrets from 'em, treacherous doings in the night and on and on until our entire brotherhood was poisoned with doubt and suspicion?

(town bell)

JEFF. Isn't that the fire bell? Odd hour for a conflagration.

WILD. My house just burned to the ground.

JEFF. Kind of late for the bell, then. We must do something to improve the fire service around here. And, please, George, no more cigars in bed. I told you an accident was bound to occur.

WILD. I wasn't at home when the fire started.

JEFF. Are you suggesting spontanious combustion?

WILD. I smelled kerosene.

JEFF. That's not good. There's a smack of arson about that.

WILD. I smell kerosene here.

JEFF. Good God, don't tell me we're next. Must be some madman loose in town. I mean, what kind of a depraved creature could ever think to burn a man's home to the ground, destroy everything he owns and cherishes. Do you have any idea who it might have been, George? *(pause)* Why you? Anyone else I might understand ... but you?

WILD. Jeff....

JEFF. Stupid, unnecessary destructive mischief. Who do you think the town would have blamed if Frank Reid's house burned down tonight, of all nights?

WILD. It would have looked like an accident.

JEFF. With kerosene stinking from hell to kingdom come.

WILD. No one could have proved a thing.

JEFF. Proof don't mean shit in the wind, George. People think with their hearts, and that kind of ugly violence would've turned every heart in this town against me.

WILD. You didn't have to do this, Jeff. You could have talked to me.

JEFF. There is some dark place inside you that words don't seem to reach. Perhaps this little fire will throw enough light on that spot so you can see to write this lesson in blood: Violence is avoided. Friendship is honored. A promise is kept. Otherwise we're all living in a jungle.

WILD. I lost everything I owned tonight.

JEFF. Empathy begets understanding. Now you know how Mr. Reid would have felt. *(pause)* Don't worry, George, I had all your belongings removed before the fire. And I'll buy you a new house in the morning. You've lost nothing at all, except a friendship you valued too little.

WILD. Jeff, just listen to me....

JEFF. No one is to lay a hand on Mr. Reid. Is that clear?!

WILD. Why the hell does he mean so much to you, anyway? I don't understand.

JEFF. Your understanding is immaterial, Mr. Wilder. The partnership is henceforth dissolved. You are my employee now, and that is *all* you are.

TRI. *(off)* Mattie's back with the girls.

JEFF. *(calls)* Send 'em in. Crank up the Victrola, George. *(pause)* Crank up the Victrola. *(WILDER obeys.)*

(MATTIE and girls enter, groggy, false high spirits. Gang quiets them and direct eyes toward WILDER.)

JEFF. Turn the record over. *(WILDER obeys.)* Start the

machine. *(WILDER obeys.)* Put the needle on. *(WILDER obeys; music, WILDER starts to go.)* Now dance, George. *(Pause. WILDER looks murderously at JEFF. Then he begins to dance oddly to the slow music. JEFF watches.)* Ain't that the saddest sight in the world? A man dancing all alone. Moving to his own music and longing for everyone to hear what he hears and join his dance. Someone help him out. *(Girl joins WILDER.)* See that. Already it's better. Two people moving together. Let's all join in. Come on, everyone, dance. *(Gang and girls come together, hesitant, puzzled.)* Dance, I said. DANCE!!! *(All dance as JEFF sits watching.)*

Scene Six

PAUL McALEER with notebook. He reads now with a more private meaning.

PAUL.
WHAT DRIVES A MAN TO FLEE HIS PAST
TO VENTURE THE UNKNOWN
WHAT HOPES HE THEN TO FIND AFAR
HE COULD NOT FIND AT HOME

PERHAPS TO MAKE HIS LIFE ANEW
OR HEAL AN ANCIENT SCAR
YET WISDOM OLD SAYS WHAT WE WERE'S
THE CHILD OF WHAT WE ARE

NO, CAST ASIDE THESE ANCIENT TRUTHS
NEW LANDS FOR NEW RULES CRY
OUR EMBLEM NOW THE NEWBORN PHOENIX
RIS'N FROM ASH ONCE MORE TO FLY
NEWBORN ONCE MORE TO FLY

Scene Seven

PAUL McALEER's room. Cubbyhole in hotel, small bed, desk by wood-burning stove. PAUL sits writing.

PAUL.
MIGHT NOT A MAN REDEEM HIMSELF
THROUGH WILL AND STRENGTH OF HEART....

(knock on door)

PAUL. Who is it?

(KITTY enters.)

KITTY. Someone needs to talk to you, Mackie. Is it all right?

(Without waiting, she brings in FRANK REID.)

KITTY. This is Frank Reid.
PAUL. Mr. Reid.

KITTY. He wants your help, Mackie. Go on, Mr. Reid.

REID. You know that Jeff Smith and his boys are getting up an army?

PAUL. I heard something about that.

REID. They aim to take over this town, and God help us all if they ever succeed. There's a good chance we can stop 'em if we can get evidence they're all working together as an organized gang.

PAUL. I'm afraid I don't know what you're talking about, Mr. Reid.

KITTY. Mackie!

REID. Kitty says you told her about a payroll list. The entire set-up. You get that to me, and the Commissioner will have a strong argument to request reinforcements, enough troops to arrest the lot of 'em in one clean sweep.

PAUL. Kitty must've misunderstood. I don't know about any gang or any list....

KITTY. Let me talk to him alone, Mr. Reid.

REID. I guess you figure you're just having a few good times with Jeff and the boys. Might've done the same at your age. But don't fool yourself, son. They're out to play for keeps. The further you get in, the less getting out there'll ever be. Remember, you got Kitty to think about now. *(exits)*

KITTY. Mackie, how could you go and lie like that?

PAUL. How could you tell him something I said to you in absolute confidence? If Jeff ever found out...

KITTY. What? Are you afraid of him?

PAUL. No! He trusts me is all. I can't let him down.

KITTY. Let him down? You don't owe him anything.

PAUL. Why all this stuff against Jeff Smith all of a sudden? He hasn't done anything to you.

KITTY. He's doing something to you, Mackie. And it's pulling you away from me.

PAUL. You don't understand about Jeff.

KITTY. What don't I understand? That he's taking over this town? That no one can escape him?

PAUL. Come on, Kitty, he gave us a fire department, the first schoolhouse in the district, and he gave your uncle a church when no one else around here would lift a finger to help...

KITTY. Yes, he helped my uncle. But I don't fool myself that he'd have done anything of the kind if it hadn't served his purposes.

PAUL. I didn't notice your uncle refusing to accept.

KITTY. Don't you dare, Mackie. My uncle is a dear and innocent man who refuses to believe ill of anyone in the world.

PAUL. Then your uncle is a fool, because everyone else in Skagway is out to line their pockets, and it sure as hell wasn't Jeff Smith who taught them how to do business.

KITTY. Stop it, Mackie. You're being cynical and stupid.

PAUL. No, you listen to me. This entire town is built on a vein of greed ten miles wide, and the only virtuous man is the one who gives back a little of what he takes and makes no excuses for what he is, and by that measure Jeff Smith is worth a thousand of anyone else around here.

KITTY. Listen to yourself, Mackie. It's all words. Only this isn't a poem. What you're doing now can't be put away in a drawer if it turns out badly. Please, Mackie, please get out of it while you can.

PAUL. Oh, so now it's me you're worried about.

KITTY. You most of all.

PAUL. Well, don't. I can take care of myself.

KITTY. For God sake, Mackie, you're no match for those people. You're a child...

PAUL. Thanks for putting me wise, Kitty, but I don't need advice about how to run my life from some overprotected, stuck-up Eastern brat.

KITTY. *(pause)* I see. Well, it's nice to know what you really think of me at last. Because sometimes it's hard for stuck-up Eastern women like myself to divine the true feelings of an uncultivated dirt farmer from Nebraska. Here is your gold heart. And here is the book of verse you gave me for Christmas. *(Gives these things.)* I enjoyed it. But allow me to give you one last piece of advice, since you've decided to travel in the company of professional deceivers. The next time you give someone a book, read it first, and make sure it doesn't contain a poem you said you wrote one month earlier, especially for her. Good day, Mr. McAleer. *(exits)*

Scene Eight

PAUL McALEER comes forward.

PAUL. And that's how I lost Kitty Chase.

(distant drum beat)

PAUL. I was new to love and didn't know a cure for heartbreak. All I had to fall back on was my poem, my magnum opus. *(drum beat louder, nearer)* I wrote in a delerium, I drank, I spent sleepless nights and watched in a kind of stupor as my hero rose to absolute mastery over the entire town. *(Strikes pose, reads loudly as drum beats approach.)*
THEY SAY THE ANCIENT WARRIOR GODS
MEN'S SOULS WITH FRENZY STIRRED
SO JEFF SMITH'S CRY OF 'DOWN WITH SPAIN'
ROUSED EVERY HEART THAT HEARD

FORSAKING EVEN DREAMS OF GOLD
THEY RALLIED TO HIS CALL
BY WINTER'S END THE COLONEL MARCHED
WITH HEAD HELD HIGH BEFORE THEM ALL
HEAD HIGH BEFORE THEM ALL

(Soldiers enter: The First Alaska Guard Volunteers [i.e. gang plus others] led by JEFF SMITH. We are at:)

Scene Nine

The Broadway. Reviewing stand center, JEFF stands on it flanked by STRONG, WHITMORE, BARKDULL, SHERPY and

REVEREND DICKEY. *Behind them, a huge American Flag and straw effigy of General Weyler suspended from pole. Several vigilantes hold flaming torches. Crowds of townspeople cheer as First Alaska Guard Volunteers complete a precision manuever and come to a halt before the reviewing stand, facing audience.*

JEFF. *(with letter)* We here in Washington are joyed to honor your newly-formed regiment of volunteers. Stand tall you Sons of Skagway, proud in your patriotic service to the Republic in This Her Time of Need. God bless America. God bless the First Alaska Guard Volunteers, and God bless my friend and patriot, Colonel Jefferson Randolph Smith. Signed, William B. McKinley, President of the United States of America. *(cheers)* My friends, Skagway is on the map!!! *(cheers)* Now I've heard some people say, "Why all this fuss about Spain, a nation seven thousand miles from our shores?" Would they take comfort in mere distance? I would ask them to remember what lies beneath Alaskan soil. I would ask them to remember what lay beneath the soil of South America when the rapacious Iberians took to their warships and sailed half the globe to massacre an entire nation of Noble Inca. You smile. You say, "But that was the Inca." Then tell me, friends, what was that Spanish gunboat doing off our coast several nights ago following our steamer, The Pride of Alaska, *with its lights off?* Mere rumor, perhaps? And detailed maps of the Klondike goldfields captured in the headquarters of the Spanish High Command? Another rumor? Well, how many rumors will it take to show us once and for all what the

Spanish are planning? The economic health of our Republic is its flow of gold from right beyond these mountains. Capture the Klondike in a daring midnight raid, and in the words of this man behind me, Spain's own great hero General Weyler, "America the Bankrupt will shrivel and fall into our hands like a dead leaf." *(Crowd roars disapproval.)* WELL LET 'EM TRY IT, THAT'S WHAT I SAY!!! *(cheers)* ARE WE READY TO GIVE THE SPANISH A ROYAL SKAGWAY WELCOME? *(cheers)* HERE'S MY MESSAGE TO GENERAL WEYLER AND ALL THE REST OF HIS GARLIC EATERS: I AM A TRUE SON OF SKAGWAY AND *THIS IS MY TOWN.* TOUCH IT AND YOU TOUCH FIRE!!! *(Fires gun in air.)*

CROWD. BURN WEYLER ... BURN WEYLER ... BURN WEYLER... *(Etc. JEFF sets fire to effigy of General Weyler with torch as crowd chants. As effigy burns, JEFF comes forward, stands facing audience with spot on face, master of Skagway. Blackout.)*

END OF ACT TWO

ACT THREE
Scene One

Back room, JEFF SMITH's Oyster Parlor. JEFF and GOVERNOR BRADY at center of a formal grouping which includes DICKEY and vigilantes (minus REID), all posed for a photographer (and assistant). JEFF holds box which contains a gold key on a bed of purple velvet. The room is hung with red, white and blue bunting. Outside, sounds of celebration ... firecrackers, cheers, a band. Gang is present, wearing crowd control bands on arm, including PAUL McALEER.

JEFF. *(formal)* On this great 4th of July, the 122nd anniversary of our Great Republic, it is my honor, on behalf of the citizens of Skagway and the First Alaska Guard Volunteers, to present you, Governor Brady, with this gold key to our city. *(Applause. JEFF and BRADY shaking hands, box with key held between them.)*

BRADY. *(formal)* Thank you, Colonel Smith. Your patriotism and military zeal have brought honor upon all of Territorial Alaska. This spring the Klondike has proven bountiful beyond our wildest dreams, and your fine town sets a shining example of enterprise, industry....

PHOTOG. Keep the hand still, Governor. It'll blur the picture if you keep pumping it up and down.

BRADY. Yes. *(lost)* Ah...

JEFF. ...enterprise ... industry...

BRADY. ...industry and ... courage, and ... and I'm proud to be the guest of honor at your ceremonies on this fine...

(Pop / flash, photo taken. Bonhomie. Enter COMISSIONER SEHLBREDE with militiaman.)

SEHL. I have the results of the election, Governor.

JEFF. Well, don't keep us in suspense, Commissioner, who is our Grand Marshall, tell us, pray?

SEHL. The results are in the envelope. *(He hands BRADY the envelope, salutes and exits with militiaman.)*

WHIT. Gentlemen, may I suggest we proceed outside to the reviewing stand so the Governor can announce the results.

BRADY. With the greatest pleasure. *(Vigilantes start outside.)*

BARK. *(exiting)* Make room for the Governor ... the Governor's coming through... *(etc.)*

JEFF. *(intercepting BRADY)* Governor, could you linger here just a moment. I've sent for the gentleman we were speaking of.

BRADY. Will we not be missed out front?

JEFF. A slight delay can only enhance the final appearance.

BRADY. By God, Colonel Smith, you have the instincts of a natural politician. You might consider a career.

JEFF. *(smiles)* Syd, get my friend Governor Brady something grown-up to drink. By the by, what was the final tally?

BRADY. *(Opens envelope.)* "Grand Marshall, Town of ... Skagway..." let me see, ah, yes, here we are... "Jared Haskell, 18; Hollis Endicott, 26; Colonel J. R. Smith, 9,182." I'd call that fairly decisive.

JEFF. *(genuine surprise)* But ... that's unanimous.

BRADY. It looks as if your career is off to a flourishing start, though the office is purely ceremonial.

JEFF. No, I mean, Sehlbrede monitored that vote. There couldn't be any hanky panky. That is the true and spontanious sentiments of the entire town.

BRADY. That's what an election means, Colonel. You seem surprised.

JEFF. May I have a little peek at that result? *(Takes list.)*

PHOTOG. I'm off, Jeff. Got to set up for the parade outside.

JEFF. By the bank. On the corner. I'll swing by right in front of you and rear up my horse, yeah, I'll wave my hat and smile, that'll make a dandy picture for the rotogravure.

(DOC JACKSON enters at front door.)

DOC. He's coming this way, Colonel.

JEFF. Let him through. Do forgive me, Governor, photopictures are my one incurable weak spot. Mackie, go saddle up my horse. *(Photographer and PAUL exit rear.)*

(REID appears in side door.)

ACT III THE BALLAD OF SOAPY SMITH 85

JEFF. Come on in, Frank, there's someone here who wants to meet you. Governor Brady, allow me to introduce you to Frank Reid.

BRADY. Mr. Reid, I've been hearing exceptional things about your dedicated work here in Skagway. *(shaking hands)*

REID. *(puzzled)* Thank you, sir. Thank you very much.

BRADY. You're of course aware that gold has put Alaska on the map this spring. Statehood is just around the corner for us, and we want to show Washington that we have men to administer such an entity, men of proven character, like yourself. With your permission I would like to offer you the post of Secretary General of American Alaska.

REID. *(pause)* Secretary General....?

BRADY. That is correct. You'll be stationed here in Skagway with troops at your disposal, and you'll be answerable to me alone. Do a good job and who knows what might lie ahead. Alaska is the future, my friend, and you can be a part of it.

REID. Isn't this a lot of confidence to put in someone you don't know?

BRADY. You have a most persuasive champion, Mr. Reid. Think it over. We'll speak before I leave. Colonel Smith, I'll be watching for you on the Broadway. *(Handshakes all around. BRADY exits. The gang remains discretely present by refreshment table while JEFF talks to REID.)*

JEFF. I expect you're wondering what's going on here.

REID. Not especially. You had words with the Governor. The Governor had words with me. And now we're having words with each other.

JEFF. You're an odd rooster, Frank. Man shows you a horse you go, "Well, it's got a horse's head, and a horse's tail and legs, guess I'll stick around and see if it's a horse."

REID. *(smiles)* May be some truth in that.

JEFF. There's truth in everything I've ever said to you. Will you have a drink?

REID. All right. If you'll join me.

JEFF. Syd. *(SYD sets up drinks.)* Take the job, Frank.

REID. *(pause)* What's your angle?

JEFF. You know, there's two kinds of blindness: Trusting too quick to see your enemies in time, and trusting too slow to see your friends. Frank, do you know who your real friends are in this town?

REID. I've had a few surprises.

JEFF. You're all alone with your hands tied. I'm offering you a knife to cut the rope. See, me and the boys here, we're not the real problem in this town. Hell, we're just a bunch of old outlaws, right, fellers?

GANG. *(amused)* Right, Jeff.

JEFF. Easy as pie to nail us for our mischief. But your vigilante friends, well, they are deeply good men, just ask 'em. And armed with that kind of selfrighteous piety they can practice any outrage and chalk it off as needful to the good of the town. They're the ones'll kill to keep the law out of here, not us. Now's your chance to go right over their heads. You clean up your side of the tracks, I'll clean up mine, and together we'll turn this town around, right, boys?

GANG. *(puzzled)* Right, Jeff.

REID. You're up to something, Jeff. Only I can't figure out what it is. Or maybe you're on the level, in which case I don't know what's making you tick. So, you see, either way I'm in the dark.

JEFF. If you don't take that job, whatever happens in this town from now on, it's on your shoulders. I don't put my ass on the line twice for no doubting fool.

REID. Why don't you take the job?

JEFF. *(pause)* Frank, have you ever done something in your past you regret so bad you just pay and pay and pay for it every day of your life?

REID. *(tense)* Why do you ask?

JEFF. Man usually puts a question because he wants to know the answer.

REID. All right, I've done a thing or two, yeah.

JEFF. I'm glad you told the truth. You see, I've known for some time about that man you killed. We are an open book to each other. But I don't judge you badly for your past. I only ask you to tell me in all honesty, would you ever do that again?

REID. No.

JEFF. Careful, Frank. Are you sure beyond all reasonable doubt that you would never repeat your former transgression?

REID. *(pause)* Not if my life depended on it.

JEFF. If I could say the same I'd take the job. But I know myself too well, and if things I've grown too fond of were put in my way again... no, I need someone to keep an eye on me. Temptation is not a creature our family could resist very well. My dear pa, he died of an over fondness for alcohol, so I know whereof I speak. *(REID has finished his whiskey. JEFF takes his empty glass and hands him his own full one.)*

REID. You want me to keep an eye on you, is that it?

JEFF. I looked out for you, didn't I? The Governor's offer is proof of that. More unlikely brothers have been each other's keeper. Power should go to those with nothing to gain. Take the job.

REID. If I do, you'll have to lead a very different kind of life here.

JEFF. That's the idea.

REID. I don't know what to make of you, Jeff.

JEFF. It's a whole new world up her. We can make things happen ain't never been seen before on earth. Equal allotments, no favors. God never dreamed a more perfect government, but I can't do it without you, Frank. Please, shake my hand and say you'll take that job, cause if you don't, I've lost the biggest gamble of my life, and this town may have to pay for it beyond all reckoning. *(His hand is out.)*

REID. Maybe I've had you wrong all along. Maybe it's time to start with a clean slate. All right, I'll take the job. *(They shake hands.)*

(PAUL rushes in.)

PAUL. Your horse is all saddled up. Better get out there quick. Parade can't start without you.

REID. Thanks for the whiskey, Jeff. Best I've had in

ages. *(Starts out.)*

JEFF. Oh, Frank, did you hear about the election? *(Shows tally sheet.)* I'm Grand Marshall. It's unanimous. You mind my asking... and be honest now... who'd you vote for?

REID. To tell the truth, I never got around to voting on that. It's just a parade, Jeff. Heck, it's just a parade. *(He exits smiling.)*

WILD. *(Comes forward with money out of pocket.)* Looks like you won yourself a friend. Here's your ten thousand.

JEFF. No, you keep your money, Mr. Wilder. George. Georgie-boy. This day is payment in full.

(Enter MATTIE SILKS, a-bustle. Outside, the crowd chants for JEFF.)

MATTIE. Hurry up, Jeff. They're going crazy for you out there. I got all my girls on a big yellow float called SPRING FEVER.

JEFF. Boys, new rules: Keep off the streets, keep off the trails, keep out of the shops. From here on in, it's law and order all the way.

DOC. But, Colonel, sir. This little trickle of miners from the heartland will soon be a mighty stream, that's the word...

SYD. Exactly, and so our question to you would have to be, "What's our game?"

JEFF. Money's what you came for, money's what you'll get. But why risk our necks when we can get it safe and legal? There'll be gold enough now for everyone to prosper by honest means. Is such abundance not a sign, my friends? Why else would the Good Lord put such an opportunity in our way?

SYD. If this is the start of a new style hustle, it sounds mighty promising.

RED. But how do we turn the con using that line?

JEFF. Is that all there is, Red? Haven't you ever dreamed of walking through the day unashamed? We all have precious years ahead of us. Why not use 'em right? Make strict rules for liquor and gaming. Set up businesses, deal straight with the trade, force those vigilante boys down to fair prices and honest dealing. Equal allotments, no favors. Just imagine if we all turned out to be the instrument of this town's deliverance, God's kingdom on earth.

BOWERS. Jeff, there's no one here but us, how come you're talking like this?

JEFF. I'm not getting through to y'all, am I. Never mind, one day you'll see the beauty of it. For the moment, let me put it into concepts you can readily understand: It has come to pass that Capitalism is the best hustle going.

BOWERS. As usual, Colonel, sir, we bow to your superior fore-thought and pre-planning.

JEFF. *(Dons white stetson.)* Escort me to my mount, would you, Mattie, dear?

MATTIE. You sure you want to be seen in public with the likes of an old reprobate like me?

JEFF. A time is coming when this town will kiss your skirts. My, but ain't it a wondrous fine day in Skagway town. Gentlemen.... *(JEFF sweeps out with a gesture for his gang to follow. PAUL goes out. RED and DOC begin to follow.*

Rest of gang lingers.)

RED. You fellers coming?

BOWERS. Would I be the only one among us haunted by the feeling that our dear friend Soapy is waxing a trifle eccentric of late?

SYD. I was struck by that very same thought, Charlie.

DOC. If he'd tell us his goddamn game, maybe we'd play.

WILD. Seems the Colonel is forgetting who his friends are. Maybe it's time we reminded him.

BOWERS. I'm intrigued by the drift of your text, Mr. Wilder. What precisely did you have in mind?

WILD. A little something to show the Colonel what this town really thinks of him once the parades have ended.

BOWERS. And thereby awaken him to his truer self. Interesting, Mr. Wilder. And the means?

WILD. Anyone care to go hunting? I'm sure there's fair game much nearer than we think.

RED. Wait a minute, you heard what Jeff said.

WILD. You want to be dancing for Mr. Reid this summer?

RED. Jeff is still running the show.

BOWERS. A condition which at this particular moment in time I find myself increasingly inclined to look upon, alas, with an attitude of Fuck Him.

SYD. Charlie has an interesting point. We sit around all winter organizing, and just when it turns out the Klondike is a monster strike, Jeff decides to play model citizen. It lacks logic.

Doc. I don't suppose we'd be missed on the Broadway.

Wild. Red, you in?

Red. *(with gun)* Well, I suppose if it's displeasing in the eyes of the Lord, he'll surely find a way to stop us. *(Gang exits.)*

Scene Two

Sixth and Broadway. Onto stage staggers J.D. STEWART, dazed, head bloody. He checks his backpack.

Stew. Where the hell is it?

Passer-By. What'd you lose, friend?

Stew. My poke. All my gold. *(Feels blood on head.)* Hell, I been sandbagged. They got my diggings.

Passer-By. You from in-country?

Stew. I just got here. I'se taking a leak, they hit me from behind, when I come to, my poke's gone. Whole winter's diggings. Three thousand dollars...

Bark. *(approaching)* What's going on here?

Passer-By. Feller's just out of the Klondike. Says he was robbed.

Bark. Where'd it happen?

Stew. Right in there...

Passer-By. That's Jeff Smith's place.

Stew. God damn this town, they warned me not to come out through here. I want my gold back. I want it back.

BARK. All right, friend, calm yourself down, we'll take care of this...

STEW. I'll head right back into the goldfields and tell 'em all about this town. Ain't no one ever gonna come out through here again....

BARK. No need to make noise, friend. We'll help you out, just come with me. *(Leads him off.)*

STEW. *(exiting)* I want my gold back, I want it back.

PASSER-BY. What's all the ruckus?

PASSER-BY. Man says he was robbed over at Jeff Smith's.

PASSER-BY. Robbery at Jeff Smith's....!!!! *(Street clears of passers-by, all talking of the robbery.)*

(Town bell begins to ring and continues into....)

Scene Three

Back room, JEFF SMITH's Oyster Parlor. JEFF sits relaxed with cigar, dictating letter to PAUL McALEER. Behind, large new photograph of JEFF and BRADY with vigilantes. Town bell rings in distance.

JEFF. "I hope your visit to Washington is proving profitable, friend Brady, and that Mr. Reid's name has met with general approval. I am yours....", etc, etc. Get that in the next post. *(calls)* TRIPOD! *(to PAUL)* Oh, post scriptum, "Warmest regards to Billy McKinley." My cousin

Bobo and he were schoolmates.

(enter TRIPOD)

JEFF. What's all that clanging outside?
TRI. I was wondering the same thing myself, Jeff. Streets seem kind of empty for this hour.
JEFF. Have some of the boys take a look around.
(TRIPOD exits rear.)

(Through front [restaurant] enter SEHLBREDE, J.B. STEWART [head bandaged], militiaman, STRONG, WHITMORE and BARKDULL.)

SEHL. Smith, this man, J.D. Stewart was robbed of three thousand dollars in gold yesterday. It happened in your saloon and I'm holding you responsible.
JEFF. Afternoon, gentlemen, is there something I can do for you?
STEW. People hereabouts been telling me all about you, Soapy Smith. It was your gang done it and I'll have satisfaction.
JEFF. Son, if you've been the victim of a crime in this town, I'll do everything in my power to help you, but lawfully. You submit a full report, name witnesses and present evidence, *then* charges will be brought. That is the correct procedure, is it not, Commissioner?
STEW. I don't need no witnesses. It happened right out there in that room. Now give me back my gold or by damn I'll head right back into the Klondike and tell'em everything they say about Soapy Smith is the God's hon-

est truth. I'll tell my story to every newspaper in the Territory. No one'll ever pass through here again, I swear to Christ....

STRONG. Steady on, friend, we'll get you back your gold.

JEFF. This man seems a trifle overwrought. Why don't you calm him down out front while I finish my correspondance with Washington.

SEHL. You have until two o'clock to return that gold, Smith.

JEFF. What happens at two o'clock?

SEHL. I'll arrest you.

JEFF. For owning a room in which a crime may or may not have taken place? Do be serious, Sehlbrede.

SEHL. You've given me the runaround up here, Smith. But yesterday you slipped and fell right into my hands. I'll make this stick, count on it.

JEFF. Go back to Dyea, Commissioner. We have law in Skagway, and our own troops to enforce it.

SEHL. *(pocket watch)* You have just over two hours. That should be sufficient.

JEFF. Get out of my office. *(They go. WHITMORE, STRONG and BARKDULL remain.)*

JEFF. Explain yourselves.

STRONG. The town is extremely alarmed about that Stewart fellow. So are we, Jeff. We've been trying to keep him quiet but he went screaming right to the top and got Sehlbrede in here.

BARK. He's one of the first men out. If word spreads back in-country he was robbed coming through Skagway ... just when all those other miners are figuring which route to bring their gold out ... we can't afford to have that happen.

JEFF. Well, neither can I, Calvin, or have you forgotten that I am in business here, too. So how do you come to be in the company of men making wild accusations?

WHIT. We don't want the law in on this, Jeff. We've got to show folks we can handle the affair ourselves.

BARK. You've always taken care of business on your side of town. Just take personal charge of getting the gold back, that's all we're asking.

JEFF. I don't understand your language, gentlemen. I happen to be a law abiding citizen of this town. *(Vigilantes exchange a look.)*

WHIT. Just talk to your gang, Jeff. Find out who done it and cough up the gold.

JEFF. My gang, Bill Whitmore? What gang is that? You mean all the people hereabouts with whom I do business? Such as yourself. And Calvin. And Jim Strong here?

STRONG. *(pause)* All right, straight talk, Jeff. We think you've been conning us all winter, keeping things quiet on the streets while you organized in secret for a big move this summer when the real gold starts coming in....

WHIT. And we'll be left with nothing....

BARK. You hand that gold back personally and we'll be satisfied you're still co-operating with us. Otherwise, we'll turn this town against you and they'll run you right out of here. And we don't want that, do we. You've been very good for us.

JEFF. Well, look what just crawled out from under a

dead log. If you all have some cute idea of singling me out to show the world how Skagway is taking it's problems in hand, may I remind you of your own considerable entanglements in my affairs, all of which I will make very very public if this situation gets the least bit messy.

WHIT. Just get the gold back, Jeff. We're all in this together.

JEFF. Then start acting like we are. No one leans on Jeff Smith. No one. Now you gentlemen will go to Commissioner Sehlbrede and make him call a public meeting where he will apologize for his lawless accusations against me. You will all three stand with him and express full support. You will return to me with a complete vote of confidence and then, and only then, will I use my best efforts to help uncover and return the gold. Good day, gentlemen.

BOWERS. *(sticking head in door)* Got a minute, Jeff?

JEFF. Certainly, Charlie. My gang was just on their way out. *(exit vigilantes)*

(enter gang, nervous)

BOWERS. Jeff, it's getting a little hairy out in the street. Ugly talk going round about a robbery or something...

JEFF. Where's the gold?!

SYD. *(pause)* We won it fair and square in a poker game.

RED. That Stewart outfit's just a piss poor loser.

BOWERS. It's the truth, Jeff, I stand before you and

swear it on all that I hold sacred...

JEFF. All you hold sacred could be hid under a rat turd. Who's bright idea was this? No one? Sort of a communal inspiration, was it? Just popped into everyone's head at once?

BOWERS. All right, all right, we made a mistake. Hell, no one ever reckoned on the town getting this lathered up over a little robbery. It ain't natural what's happening out there.

JEFF. One of the first men out of the Klondike and you never reckoned??!! What the hell did you reckon, Charlie? Right in my own saloon? That ain't carelessness, gentlemen, that's treachery, but that I look at you all and see stupidity deep enough to never reckon the consequences.

(TRIPOD enters.)

TRI. Jeff, all the shops are shutting down. And there's a big old crowd of folks gathered over to 4th listening to anyone who talks up.

JEFF. Go out there and keep your eye peeled. I want to know everything that's happening out there. *(Exit TRIPOD. JEFF faces gang.)* All right, gentlemen, any more bright ideas?

WILD. Just give 'em back the gold, Jeff.

SYD. Hell, yeah, it's hid near by, no problem.

DOC. We could say we took up a collection...

RED. Sure, The Jeff Smith Miner's Relief Fund...

BOWERS. Now that's what I call one hell of a righteous idea.

JEFF. Anyone who makes so much as a move to return that gold will be found floating belly-up in the Lynn Canal.

WILD. Jeff, this is no time for a game of nerves. All our asses are in the fire. Long as the gold's missing they got an issue. Give it back and the whole thing'll blow over in a day or two....

JEFF. THEY CAME TO ME, GOD DAMN IT. *THEY CAME TO ME!!!* After all I've done for this god-forsaken shithole. No. If the gold re-appears now, it says they fingered the right man. I have my reputation to consider.

WILD. Stop it, Jeff. All the friends you have in the world are standing right here in this room. We're with you if you're with us, but you gotta drop this reputation game, cause you're getting us nervous as hell.

JEFF. *(pause)* You think my reputation is a game?

WILD. For Christ sakes open your eyes, Soapy. This whole town sees through your act. They're with you for the good times, but they know what you are. Your reputation doesn't exist. It's nothing but a lot of crazy horseshit floating around inside your head and nowhere else. *(Pause. JEFF slowly opens drawer of roll top desk. WILDER has no time to react before JEFF removes a revolver and shoots him through the heart. WILDER reels back and falls dead.)*

JEFF. *(pause)* Is there anyone else in this room who thinks my reputation is a lot of crazy horseshit?

BOWERS. *(pause)* I feel bad as hell about this, Jeff. We tried so hard to talk him out of robbing that gold...

SYD. It's true, Jeff. Almost uncanny how justice come out by pure chance. Guilty party found and executed...

Doc. I suppose we ought to turn him over to the town. With the gold on his person.

Jeff. Bury him in the woods. And bring me the gold. It will not be seen again until my name is cleared.

(TRIPOD enters.)

Tri. Jeff, I tried to listen in over to 4th but they called me one of your men and kicked the crutches right out from under me. Imagine treating an old cripple like that. *(sees)* Say, what happened to George?

Jeff. *(pacing)* Get some of the boys to break up that meeting. Use new people no one knows are with me. No violence. Just get things confused. Start it round that I'm in touch with Washington. Say that Stewart had no gold, you know the hee-haw. Sam, you know where Mr. Reid lives?

Sam. Sam know.

Jeff. Tell him I have urgent need of his assistance. And get some fellers to guard this place. Arm 'em. Arm 'em good. *(re WILDER)* Now get him out of my sight. Move it! *(Gang carries out WILDER. Only JEFF and PAUL McALEER remain.)* You better burn the payroll list, Mr. Poet. Sehlbrede and Company may pay us a scrutinizing visit. Top right hand drawer. And pour us a drink while you're at it. Listen to all that ringing. Four days ago they cheered me through the streets. I never misjudge a crowd. Their enthusiasm was real.

Paul. *(with glass)* Here's your whiskey.

Jeff. Funny thing is, the man who led their parade, Colonel Smith, benefactor of the town ... that's who I

ACT III THE BALLAD OF SOAPY SMITH 101

truely am. If they saw something different ... how sad ... the crowd ain't never wrong. *(to PAUL, re glass)* Your hand is trembling, Mr. Poet.

PAUL. I've never seen a man killed before.

JEFF. And I've never killed one. *(Holds his hand out flat, palm down. PAUL, understanding, places glass on top of it.)* Dear Lord Jesus, how could it be so easy to murder your best friend. I don't feel a thing. Not a thing. Leave me alone now. *(Exit PAUL, frightened. JEFF walks with glass on back of hand, fascinated by his own calm. Town bell stops ringing suddenly. Eerie silence. JEFF notices. His hand starts to shake. He grabs glass, drinks it down. Pours another. Drinks it. Pours another.)*

Scene Four

Town meetings and street in Skagway. The first meeting, MAJOR STRONG is the speaker, SHERPY beside him.

STRONG. Why did Jeff Smith spend the winter winning our support and confidence? So he could secretly organize a gang of thugs and sharpers under our very nose, and come summer launch a wild spree of robbery and brigandage the likes of which has never been seen before on earth, and this Stewart incident is only a small taste of things to come....

MAN 1. *(in crowd)* Major Strong is being paid by Dyea businessmen to ruin Skagway. They're trying to shut this town down.... *(uproar)*

STRONG. Who said that? Where is the man who said that?

MAN 2. *(in crowd)* Jeff has word from Governor Brady in Washington. Brady says the Colonel should deal with this business and no one else... *(uproar)*

STRONG. Who is that man??? Who let him in here???!!!

Second meeting, WHITMORE is the speaker, J.D. STEWART beside him.

WHIT. This man's gold is stolen in Jeff Smith's saloon, but does he help us get it back? No, he puts a gang of armed holligans around his place and dares us to come and get him....

MAN 3. *(in crowd)* That Stewart boy didn't have no gold. The whole thing was a set-up.... *(uproar)*

STEW. *(yelling)* WHO SAYS I HAD NO GOLD? I HAD THREE THOUSAND DOLLARS WORTH...!!!

MAN 4. *(in crowd)* You're a liar, Stewart. You didn't find no gold in the Klondike and now you're trying to make us pay for your bad luck... *(uproar)*

STEW. You come up here and say that..!!!

MAN 5. *(in crowd)* You come down here and say that... *(uproar)*

WHIT. Quiet down .... stop it down there ... order, order...!!!

ACT III   THE BALLAD OF SOAPY SMITH   103

Third meeting, SEHLBREDE as speaker, BARKDULL and STRONG with him.

MAN 6. *(in crowd)* Deputize every able-bodied man and take Jeff's saloon by force... *(uproar)*
SEHL. *(Shouts over noise.)* NO!!! I WILL NOT DEPUTIZE A MOB AND RISK INNOCENT BLOOD. You must give me time to send for reinforcements. The law will handle this...
MAN 7. *(in crowd)* Colonel Smith can handle it with his army, we don't need the damn militia....
SEHL. His army is a sham and everyone knows it. Please, people, I need your vote to bring the militia in...
MAN 8. *(in crowd)* I move that Commissioner Sehlbrede's request is out of order....
MAN 6. That's one of Jeff Smith's men....
MAN 8. You're one of Jeff Smith's men...
MAN 7. I move that this whole meeting is out of order... *(Crowd in uproar. SEHLBREDE yells above them but cannot regain control.)*

A street. Enter KITTY, followed by PAUL McALEER, who carries carpetbag.

PAUL. Stop, Kitty, I have to talk to you.
KITTY. We have nothing to say to each other, please stop following me.
PAUL. I'm leaving tonight, Kitty. I want to say good-

bye.

KITTY. *(stops)* I see. *(hard)* Well, then, good-bye. *(starts out)*

PAUL. Kitty, please listen to me. We may never see each other again. Don't think badly of me for what I said to you. God knows you're the only thing I care about that's happened to me in this town.

KITTY. What do you want from me, Mackie? My forgiveness?

PAUL. No, Kitty. I only want you to understand. I knew what I was getting into. I'll pay for that in my own way. But I never meant anything bad to come to you.

KITTY. Mackie, something's happened. What is it?

PAUL. I can't explain now. I owe him his poem. He's expecting me.

KITTY. Tell me what's going on, Mackie. Are you in danger?

PAUL. He's mad. I just saw him do something. His eyes. I saw it in his eyes, Kitty.

KITTY. You can't go back to him, Mackie. Come with me, I'll help you.

PAUL. He has people everywhere. I can't hide from Jeff Smith. And I don't want to. I have a debt to pay. I accepted it, and I'll answer for it whatever the cost. Take this *(Hands paper to her.)* ...read it as soon as you can and you'll understand how I feel about Jeff Smith. Forgive me, Kitty. *(He exits. KITTY unfolds paper, looks it over, exits quickly.)*

Scene Five

Street near JEFF SMITH's place. Enter crowd of armed men. FRANK REID enters opposite and confronts them.

REID. Where you fellers headed?
MAN 1. To Jeff Smith's. We're gonna shoot our way in and bring him out, guards or no.
REID. Just turn and head back where you came from. Reinforcements are on their way from Juneau, they'll be here in the morning. The law's going to handle this.
MAN 2. We ain't waiting for no reinforcements. This here's town business.
REID. No one is going to lose his life over some wild accusation about a robbery.
MAN 3. Who's talking about a robbery? Jeff Smith killed a man and he's gonna pay for it.
REID. Killed? Who said he killed a man?
MAN 3. We got witnesses, now stand aside, Frank Reid.
REID. Jeff Smith is not a murderer.
MAN 4. Couple of his gang seen it happen. Syd Dixon and Charlie Bowers. We got 'em under guard over to the Burkhart Hotel.
REID. Syd Dixon and Charlie Bowers? And you're ready to get yourself blown apart on the word of two lying

hoodlums? Where's your damn sense?

MAN 2. They ain't lying, Frank. They swore it up and down.

REID. I want to talk to these witnesses of yours. Take me to 'em.

MAN 1. Get out of our road, Frank. *(Points rifle.)*

REID. *(Moves rifle aside.)* No one's going anywhere until I've questioned your witnesses.

MAN 1. *(pause)* All right, see for your own damn self. Take him to the Burkhart... *(Crowd exits with REID.)*

Scene Six

Back room, JEFF SMITH's Oyster Parlor. JEFF, quite drunk now, reads aloud from PAUL's notebook. MATTIE and PAUL listen, along with TRIPOD and TAGISH SAM, who stand by.

JEFF.
THUS ENDS MY BALLAD OF A MUCH LOVED MAN
HIS HEART WAS GOOD AS GOLD
SING OUT HIS NAME WHEN E'ER THE TALE
OF SKAGWAY TOWN BE TOLD

SO THAT HIS GLORY YET SHINE FORTH
AND MEMORY NEVER FADE
AND THROUGH ALL TIME JEFF SMITH BE KNOWN

AS THE MAN WHO SKAGWAY MADE....
....The End....

PAUL. *(as TRIPOD and MATTIE applaud)* Do you like it?

JEFF. Like it? Do I like it? Mr. Poet, never in all my days as a reading man have I ever encountered such an explosion, such an erruption, such a feverish and torrential out-pouring of pure, unmitigated, prime-A-number-one rhyming flapdoodle. *(Laughs uproariously.)*

MATTIE. Aw, Jeff, it wun't all that bad. I kinda liked it, myself.

JEFF. Bad is not the word, Mattie. It opens vistas of awfulness never before glimpsed in the history of literature. *(PAUL, upset, stands.)* Aw, can't you take a little kidding, son? I like it fine. I liked it as well as anything I've ever said in *my* life. *(pause)* I'll miss you, Mackie. I don't suppose there's any chance I could talk you into staying on.

PAUL. I have other plans, Jeff.

JEFF. Well, then, let's have one last farewell toast and send you on your way.

MATTIE. No more, Jeff. You've had enough and then some.

JEFF. *(Pours generously.)* You leave me alone you terrible old woman you. Can't I loosen my belt for once and relax in this fine town of mine.

(DICKEY enters, agitated.)

DICKEY. Colonel Smith, are you aware that a full town meeting is convened at Sperry's Warehouse?

JEFF. Thank you, Reverend, that situation is well in hand.

DICKEY. I think you underestimate the degree of sentiment that's forming against you down there. I don't pretend to fully grasp what's happening, but I beg you to accept my offer of help.

(SHERPY enters, also alarmed.)

SHERPY. Jeff, I've just come from the meeting at Sperry's. It's getting very dangerous. I think you should go to them and tell them your side of the story.

JEFF. I'm waiting here for an apology, Mike. Until it comes, my men will act on my behalf.

SHERPY. Your men can't get into that meeting. They're being turned away at the foot of the dock.

JEFF. That's not possible, Mike. I sent all new faces down there. No one knows they're my men.

SHERPY. The guards have a list. They're turning your people away with no mistakes.

JEFF. A list? *(pause)* The list of my people? All my people?

SHERPY. It looks that way.

JEFF. *(figuring)* Tripod, have the boys storm Sperry's from all sides. Use anything they have to to break up that meeting.

SHERPY. They won't get near it. Sperry's is way out over the water and the entire causeway's heavily guarded.

JEFF. Mike, I am trying to spend a quiet night with my friends here. All this is upsetting me terribly.

SHERPY. Just talk to them, Jeff. It'll show 'em you're

ACT III THE BALLAD OF SOAPY SMITH 109

willing to co-operate, cause otherwise they're liable to come up here armed and there'll be a bloodbath.

JEFF. Where's Frank Reid? Didn't I send for him? Yes, I'm sure I did. Tripod, let's get this thing organized. Go find Mr. Reid. *(exit TRIPOD)*

SHERPY. I thought you knew.

JEFF. You thought I knew what?

SHERPY. Reid's at the meeting. He's one of the speakers.

JEFF. *(pause)* But he's a friend of mine. We have a very special understanding. He must be speaking in my defense, isn't that right?

SHERPY. *(carefully)* He's trying to calm things down.

JEFF. Well, there you are, he's guarding my safety. My God, what a fine man he is. Tell the multitudes I shall come among them shortly and answer their accusations. And do convey my appreciation to Mr. Reid for his efforts on my behalf this night. *(exit SHERPY)*

DICKEY. I think it would be very unwise to go down there, Colonel. There is a rage in these people tonight. Your presence will only provoke them further. Please, take this steamer ticket and leave town immediately. I used church funds, God forgive me, but after all you've done, I'm sure He will understand.

JEFF. *(taking ticket)* Thank you, Reverend. This is a kindness I'll not soon forget.

DICKEY. Say what they will, Colonel, I find you a most remarkable man. "Let he who is without sin cast the first stone."

JEFF. Amen to that.

DICKEY. God go with you. *(Exits. MATTIE signals PAUL*

to slip out behind DICKEY. He takes bag and starts to follow.)

JEFF. *(back to PAUL)* Leaving already, Mr. Poet? I haven't paid you yet. *(turns)* Why would a man be so anxious to run off before he received his just desserts?

PAUL. Right. $750, was it?

JEFF. Beautiful. A treacherous heart and the face of an angel. That's a promising combination. Why, with my brains and your pen, I bet we could bend the truth into shapes never before seen on earth. How about you join me on the next steamer? We'll find us a new town, set up shop, you and me, fifty-fifty.

PAUL. I'm not a criminal, Jeff.

JEFF. Surely you give yourself far too little credit.

PAUL. You don't see anything beyond what you can use in a man. All the rest is a complete mystery.

JEFF. If what you say is true, Mr. Poet, and I have no further use for you, what do you suggest I do with the bones of a betrayer?

PAUL. I guess you get rid of me. Isn't that what you do to anyone who doesn't buy your dream? *(pause)* Goodbye, Mattie. *(He takes up bag and starts out. JEFF grabs gun and points it at him.)*

MATTIE. No, Jeff!!

PAUL. *(Freezes, back to JEFF.)* Go ahead. I gave them the list.

JEFF. Look me in the eye, boy. *(PAUL turns.)* Very good, Mr. McAleer. There may be the makings of a man in you after all. I'm going to give you a little present. It ain't much, but you may make something of it one day if you ever learn it's true value.

PAUL. What is it?

JEFF. *(Gives one bullet from gun.)* The rest of your life, Mr. Poet, remember me and use it well. *(exit PAUL)* Sam, tell the boys to get into uniform. We'll approach the docks in full patriotic colors, and I shall stand beside my dear friend Frank Reid and address my town. The ministry trained me well for such occasions.

SAM. Boys not here. Gone to woods. Gone to mountains. Animal smell fire, run-run damn quick.

JEFF. What is it about me that inspires such loyalty? Sam, hadn't you better head for the hills with all the others?

SAM. You pay to Friday, Sam work to Friday.

JEFF. Sam, Sam, Sam, we must do something to cure you of your savage ways. *(pause)* Oh, Mattie, all I ever wanted was everything. Is that too much to ask?

MATTIE. Go, Jeff. Catch that steamer. Lay low somewhere till this blows over. I'll write you when it's safe to return.

JEFF. I wish all the way to hell I didn't see so god-awful clearly the thing I really am. Pay no mind, Mattie, that's the liquor talking. Why, those are my people out there. My town is waiting for me.

MATTIE. Don't be a damn fool. Get out while you can.

JEFF. Steak and beans for dinner, Mattie. And set three places, Mr. Reid will be joining us. Hell, if a crowd can see my eyes, I can sell 'em damn near anything on earth. *(at door, calling)* FRANK REID! WHERE IS MY FRIEND, FRANK REID??!! *(exits, yelling)*

Scene Seven

The causeway. Narrow wooden pier leading out over water to Sperry's Warehouse, partly visible at edge of stage. Guards line causeway. Enter JEFF with revolver drawn, swaying slightly.

JEFF. *(calling)* FRANK REID, WHERE ARE YOU? COME ON OUT AND LEAD ME IN. I WANT TO ADDRESS MY PEOPLE WITH MY FRIEND FRANK REID BY MY SIDE.

(Guards part as FRANK REID appears in door of Sperry's, a crowd pressing out behind him.)

JEFF. Frank, I've come here in all humility to offer my explanation.
GUARD. Careful, Frank, he's armed. *(GUARD hands REID a rifle.)*
REID. The town had a vote. They want you in jail.
JEFF. But I haven't spoken yet. That's hardly fair. Tell 'em they have to listen to me, Frank, tell 'em.
REID. You and me had an understanding. You broke it.
JEFF. You don't believe I took that gold, do you?
REID. That's not what I mean.

JEFF. I'm innocent till proven otherwise. I demand a hearing.

REID. Two of your men say you murdered George Wilder. Should I believe 'em?

JEFF. I only tell you the truth, Frank. Always. Yes, I killed George Wilder. But you mustn't think badly of me. It was self-defense. He attacked my reputation, you see. What else does a man have?

REID. It's all over, Jeff. I can't help you any more. I'm taking you to the jailhouse.

JEFF. Why so cold, Frank? I've given you everything. My trust. My respect. Power. All I ever asked in return was your good opinion. Give me that and I'll be whatever you say. We need each other, don't you see that? Together, my God, what a town we could make here. A new land. A place to start again. You know I meant that when you shook my hand. God in Heaven, you have to believe me because I've never told you anything but the deepest truth in my heart. Look at me, Frank, look me in the eye. Can't you see it?

REID. All I see is a con man who's conned himself, and it's a sorry damn sight.

JEFF. *(Fires gun. Click.)* ...Mr. Poet...? No, Frank...!!! *(FRANK REID fires, then JEFF. Both fall.)*

GUARD. *(Goes to JEFF's body, feels for pulse.)* Soapy's dead. He's dead, start rounding up his gang... *(This call is taken up by all as they run off stage. REID's body is taken out by guards. BARKDULL, STRONG nad WHITMORE check JEFF's body, take his gun, nod to each other and walk to back of stage where they freeze.)*

(PAUL enters, walking between them to where JEFF lies in a pool of light.)

Scene Eight

PAUL McALEER. He addresses us.

PAUL. Jeff died instantly, shot clean through the heart. Frank Reid passed away several days later from loss of blood. Thus ended the reign of Soapy Smith. He was buried under a plain yellow pine marker that reads: **HERE LIE THE BONES OF SOAPY SMITH / THE GETTING WAS EASY / THE KEEPING A BITCH.**

One final irony. The Klondike strike went dry in a couple of summers. Yeah, it was a flash in the pan, and all those busy merchants who lived off the miners like blood ticks off a cow's back, they all went bust.

As for Jeff's gift? *(Takes bullet from pocket.)* Well, I lived a quiet life and died peaceful in bed, Kitty by my side and children to mourn me. But I went to my grave with a restless soul. See, I could never shake out of my mind this one image of Jeff Smith as the man he wanted to become ... the man in my poem. And I'll always wonder if he might've got there if we'd all just believed in him a little more. It's hard to be anything without a little confirmation from outside.

And that's my story. While I lived in Skagway I wrote Jeff's dream. Tonight I showed you what really happened. Now I can rest in peace for my sins. I wish the same to you one day, my friends. *(He turns and exits. SOAPY SMITH lies dead in a pool of light. Fade.)*

END OF ACT THREE

THE END

PROPERTIES PRESET ONSTAGE

ACT ONE

Baggage Cart with
- Oars
- Trunk
- Whiskey flask
- Blanket
- Tarp

SR Tower with
- Break-a-way bottle
- Whiskey bottle & glass

ACT TWO

2 cots with blankets and pillows
Small table with
- Thermometer
- Record book
- Pencil
- Bottle

Chair with rag (round back)
Platform with pulpit
Pew

ACT THREE

Banquet table (without false top)
Roll top desk with
- Letter paper, Bot & 2 glasses
- Pen
- Inkwell
- Soapy's & George's hats

top right — list of gang
　　　right desk drawer — Soapy's gun (loaded)
Straight back chair

STAGE LEFT

Gold dust bag
Money pouch
Reporter's pad & pencil
3 bunches of flowers
Rope
Gag
Blindfold
Playing cards (perishable)
Deck of playing cards
Hunting knife (Reid)
6 party glasses
2 bar cloths
4 beers
4 whiskey glasses
Whiskey bottle
Raffle tickets
Money
Kerosene can
Champagne glass
Champagne bottle
Snare drum and sticks
Torch
Camera & flash unit
Envelope with election results
10,000 cash
Steamer ticket

Coffee cup
Coffee pot
Matches
Cigars
Cross on string
Tray with 2 gift bottles
Tools and apron
2 sets knee pads
Back pad
Poker chips
Tools and apron
Ledger and pencil
Torch
Laundry basket
Basket of fruit
2 packages
Flowers (Reid)
Walking stick
Handbill
3 rifles (1 fires)
Shotgun — loaded

ACT ONE
Bar Unit with
(top)
    Tray
    Coffee pot (pract)
    Creamer
    Sugarer
    Ashtray
    2 napkins

    2 spoons
    2 cups & saucers
    tarp
(below)
    Model — boot with gun
    6 whiskey
    4 gift bottles
    Bar cloth
    Poet's tray
    2 whiskey bottles
    Apron, Haig & Haig bottle
Soapy's Trunk with moving strap and
    Faro
    Dice
    Markers
Roulette wheel
Haig & Haig bottle
Tie
Waistcoat
Jacket
8 chairs — (2 straight)

ACT TWO
Square table with 2 chairs on top
Round table
8 chairs
Chaise
Gramaphone table with gramaphone and records

ACT THREE
Swivel chair in upstage doorway

STAGE RIGHT

Key to city
Camera and flash unit
Steamer tickets
Money
Sandwich board
Hunting knife (Chinn)
Bucket with bottles and snowshoe
2 parasols
6 single bullets
List of criminals
Cheroots
Matches
4 party glasses
Letter to editor
Coin purse
Money purse
Paper with two names
Bar cloth
Coffee cup
Some silverware
Heart box with poem
Bone bag with bones
4 whiskey glasses
Tray with 2 whiskey, 2 beer
Tray with whiskey bottle, 2 beer
Champagne glass
Letter from President
Raffle tickets
Big ledger and money
Double notebook

Fan
Prayer book
Poet's carpet bag
Newspaper
Poetry volume
Heart on long chain
3 bundles
3 carpet & shopping bags
$500.00 bill (personal)
Wad of cash (Soapy)
Jensen's miner's pack with wallet
Torch
Effigy
Backsack, miner's pack
Coffin
Shovel
Bible
Packages
Fruit basket
Soapy's gun — loaded
5 pistols — unloaded
    Wilder
    Whitmore
    Bowers
    Doc
    Burke
2 pistols — loaded
    Syd
    Red
3 rifles

ACT ONE
Rectangular table
Square table with cloth
Banquet table with extension and cloth
6 chairs (2 straight)
Counter with cash register
    2 dusters
    Stool

ACT TWO
Rectangular table
3 chairs (round back)

ACT THREE
Chaise
Gramaphone table with book on bottom

COSTUME PLOT

WORKMAN, BURKE GALLAGHER, COMMISSIONER SEHLBREDE
ACT ONE, SCENE ONE
WORKMAN
Brown corduroy pants
Suspenders
Blue plaid distressed shirt
Cuffless brown boots
Tie (paisley print)
Green pea coat
Brown fedora
T-shirt
Black socks
Brown boots
ACT ONE, SCENE FIVE
BURKE GALLAGHER
Remove pants / suspenders
Remove Green peacoat
Remove brown fedora
Rust / brown plaid pants
Rust / brown plaid jacket
Red / brown / beige tweed vest
Brown derby
ACT TWO, SCENE ONE
SEHLBREDE
Remove all Burke Gallagher
Dk. Grey Tailcoat

Black wool pants
Suspenders
Black wool vest
Grey stripe shirt
White collar
Blue / black print tie
Black fedora
Black riding boots
ACT TWO, SCENE NINE
Remove tailcoat
Remove black fedora
Green peacoat
Brown fedora
ACT THREE, SCENE ONE
SEHLBREDE
Black fedora
Tailcoat, dr. grey

"RED" GIBBS
ACT ONE, SCENE ONE
Distressed leather jacket
Beige / purple turtleneck sweater
Mauve jodhpurs with suspenders
Black riding boots
Tweed newsboy cap
Beige wallace berky
Black socks
Brown leather belt
ACT TWO, SCENE NINE
Remove all Gibb costume
Grey militia tunic

Black jodhpurs
Black riding boots
Brown Sam Brown belt
Black Mounty hat
ACT THREE, SCENE ONE
Remove militia costume
Act One, Scene One — basic Gibbs costume
Red arm band
ACT THREE, SCENE TWO
Remove red arm band

FRENCHIE / MINER / MILITIA / TOWNSPERSON
ACT ONE, SCENE ONE
TOWNSPERSON
Black / brown tweed pants with suspenders
Wallace Beery shirt
T shirt
Brown suede jacket with fringe
Black belt
Red / black checked overjacket
Riding boots
Black fur hat
Black socks
Bicycle pants
ACT ONE, SCENE TWO
Blindfold
Mouth gag
Hand ties
ACT TWO, SCENE THREE
Remove all clothing except socks and shirt
Harness / felt pad

Elbow pads
Noose
Distressed fringed jacket
Pants
Wallace Beery shirt
Belt
Boots
Red / plaid jacket
Black fur hat
ACT TWO, SCENE SEVEN
Remove all Frenchie costume
Wader boots
Grey tweed pants with suspenders
Black belt
Brown wool tweed shirt
Gloves
Bandanna
Knit cap, brown
ACT TWO, SCENE NINE
Remove all miner costume
Grey military costume
Black jodhpurs with suspenders
Black riding boots
Sam Brown belt
Black Mounty hat
ACT THREE, SCENE ONE
TOWNSPERSON
Remove all militia costume
Grey pants with suspenders
Dark purple stripe shirt
Tweedy brown vest

Grey tweed coat
Brown felt hat
Grey distressed boots

DOC JACKSON
ACT ONE, SCENE ONE
Blue frock coat
Red / black paisley tie
Wingtip collar
Black / gold / white stripe shirt
Blue tweed vest with watch fob
Blue & lt. grey stripe pants
Suspenders
Black high top boots
Black derby
ACT TWO, SCENE FOUR
Remove frock coat
ACT TWO, SCENE SIX
Remove collar
Grey Military tunic
Overcoat, blue wool
ACT TWO, SCENE EIGHT
Remove overcoat
Remove pants
Remove black hightop boots
Black jodhpurs
Black riding boots
Mounty hat
Sam Brown belt
ACT THREE, SCENE ONE
Remove all militia costume

Doc Jackson basic (Act One, Scenes I & II)
Red arm band
ACT THREE, SCENE TWO
Remove frock coat, tie, vest, collar
Frock coat

BARKDULL
ACT ONE, SCENE ONE
Black pants with suspenders
Duster with hood
Brown stripe shirt
Black socks
T-shirt
ACT ONE, SCENE SIX A
Remove duster and hood
Collar (wingtip)
Tie
Black vest with watch fob
Black frock coat
Duster with hood
ACT ONE, SCENE SIX
Remove duster and hood
Black Homberg
ACT ONE, SCENE EIGHT
Remove Homberg
ACT TWO, SCENE ONE
Overcoat
Homberg
ACT TWO, SCENE NINE
Gloves

ACT THREE, SCENE ONE
Remove gloves and overcoat
Black top hat
ACT THREE, SCENE TWO
Remove top hat
Homberg

MAJOR JAMES STRONG
ACT ONE, SCENE ONE
White shirt / collar
Blue brocade cravat with ruby stickpin
Black frock coat
Black vest with watch fob
Black pants with suspenders
Grey duster with hood
Black hightop boots
Black socks
T-shirt
ACT ONE, SCENE EIGHT
Remove duster & hood
ACT TWO, SCENE ONE
Overcoat
Gloves
Homberg
ACT TWO, SCENE NINE
Remove gloves
ACT THREE, SCENE ONE
Remove overcoat, gloves, Homberg
Black top hat
ACT THREE, SCENE TWO B
Remove top hat

Black Homberg

TAGISH SAM
ACT ONE, TWO, THREE
Red plaid shirt
3 piece greenish/brown small plaid suit with green suspenders
Black fedora
Dark brown fur coat
Brown boots
Acorn and wood necklace
T-shirt
Black socks

FRITZ
ACT ONE, TWO, THREE
Distressed dark beige tail coat
Distressed brown tweed pants
Distressed embroidered "Alps" suspenders
Distressed tweed shirt
Distressed black felt hat
T-shirt
Black socks

SHERPY & MINER
ACT ONE, SCENE ONE
SHERPY
Black vest
Blue / white stripe collarless shirt
Collar — rounded, white
Brown paisley tie

Duster with hood
Grey suit pants with suspenders
T-shirt
Black socks
ACT ONE, SCENE SIX
Remove duster and hood
Grey Suit jacket
Black Homberg
ACT ONE, SCENE EIGHT
Remove Homberg
ACT TWO, SCENE TWO
Remove all Sherpy
Distressed grey shirt
Red / gold plaid shirt
Distressed brown / beige wool pants with checked suspenders
Dark brown wool jacket
Brown boots
Knit brown wool hat
ACT TWO, SCENE FOUR
Remove all miner
Act I — Scene I Sherpy
Dark grey overcoat
Black Homberg
Grey stripe scarf
ACT TWO, SCENE NINE
Gloves
ACT THREE
Remove overcoat, gloves, scarf

TRIPOD SCHULTZ
ACT ONE, TWO, THREE
Brown plaid pants with suspenders
Tan Wallace Beery Shirt
Brown shirt (knit)
Grey, black, red stripe vest
Raw silk / rubber overcoat
Black cowboy hat
1 brown aged boot
1 wrestling shoe with D-ring

REV. CHARLIE BOWERS
ACT ONE, SCENE ONE
3-piece black mohair suit
Black suspenders
Black shirt
Black flat-top hat
Black high-top boots
Black socks
T-shirt
ACT ONE, SCENE EIGHT
Remove hat and suit coat
ACT TWO, SCENE TWO
Hat
Suitcoat
Overjacket, black / brown
Scarf
ACT TWO, SCENE FIVE
Gloves
ACT THREE, SCENE ONE
Remove overcoat, scarf, gloves

Red arm band and button
ACT THREE, SCENE TWO
Remove red arm band

TOWNSPERSON / MINER / GOV. BRADY
ACT ONE, SCENE ONE
TOWNSPERSON
Brown tweed coat
Rust / grey / gold / plaid pants
Green suspenders
Brown brocade vest
Grey / yellow / black / red stripe cavalry shirt
Black high-top cavalry boots
Brown derby
Black socks
T-shirt
ACT TWO, SCENE TWO
MINER
Remove brown tweed coat
Remove brown derby
Remove brown brocade vest
Remove black high-top boots
Wool leggings
Brown boots
Black distressed fedora
ACT TWO, SCENE NINE
TOWNSPERSON
Remove leggings
Remove boots
Remove black distressed fedora
Brown brocade vest

Brown derby
Brown tweed jacket
ACT THREE, SCENE ONE
GOV. BRADY
Remove all townsperson
Black pants with suspenders
White collarless shirt
Wing-tip collar
Mauve vest with watch fob
Black high-top boots
Black frock coat
Black top hat
ACT THREE, SCENE FIVE
Remove all Gov. Brady except shoes
Townsperson — (Act I — Scene I)

WHORE / TOWNSPERSON
ACT ONE, SCENE ONE
Pink & white corset
White eyelet bloomers
Black stockings & garters
Black lace-up shoes
Rust plaid blouse
White petticoat
Rust jacket & skirt
Black hat
Rust velvet belt
ACT ONE, SCENE THREE
Remove rust plaid blouse
Remove rust jacket & skirt
Remove rust velvet belt

THE BALLAD OF SOAPY SMITH

Black dress with satin ruffle
Plaid cape with lamb collar
ACT ONE, SCENE FOUR
Remove Plaid cape with lamb collar
Remove black hat
Black felt bonnet
Glasses
ACT TWO, SCENE TWO
Remove black dress with satin ruffle
Remove black felt bonnet
Remove glasses
Blue & black "Dance Hall" dress
Mauve neck ribbon
ACT TWO, SCENE FIVE
Remove blue & black "Dance Hall" dress
Remove Mauve neck ribbon, petticoat
Plaid cape with lamb collar
Blue velvet kimono
ACT TWO, SCENE SEVEN
Remove plaid cape with lamb collar
Remove blue velvet kimono
Light blue blouse
Green jacket & skirt, petticoat
Black hat
Chenille shawl
Cameo & wedding ring
ACT THREE
Remove light blue blouse
Remove green jacket & skirt
Remove black hat
Remove chenille shawl

Blue & white striped blouse & skirt
Blue & white striped belt
Straw hat
Cameo

WHORE / TOWNSPERSON
ACT ONE SCENE ONE
Pink corset
White eyelet bloomers
White eyelet camisole
Black stockings
Black lace-up boots
Grey skirt
White petticoat
Grey coat
Black straw hat
Black gloves
Wedding ring
Garters
ACT ONE, SCENE FIVE
Maroon and black evening dress and jacket
ACT ONE
Remove grey skirt
Remove grey coat
Remove black gloves & black straw hat
Black feathered bonnet
Chain earrings
ACT TWO, SCENE TWO
Remove maroon & black evening dress & jacket
Remove chain earrings
Remove black feathered bonnet

Remove white eyelet camisole
Remove wedding ring
Purple & black "Dance Hall" bodice & skirt
Feather hair decoration
ACT TWO, SCENE FIVE
Remove purple & black "Dance Hall" bodice & skirt
Remove white petticoat
Remove feather hair decoration
White eyelet camisole
Purple cape
Blue chiffon kimono
ACT TWO, SCENE NINE
Remove purple cape
Remove blue chiffon kimono
Grey skirt
White petticoat
Grey coat
Black straw hat & black gloves
Wedding ring
ACT THREE
Remove grey skirt
Remove grey coat
Remove black straw hat & black gloves
Blue & white striped blouse & skirt
Tan straw hat

KITTY STRONG
ACT ONE, SCENE THREE
Green corset
White eyelet camisole
2 white petticoats

Black stockings & garters
Black lace-up shoes
Beige herringbone jacket & skirt
Rust belt & watch pin
Blue with pink stripe blouse with ribbon
Plaid shawl & brown gloves
ACT ONE, SCENE FOUR
Remove plaid shawl & brown gloves
ACT TWO, SCENE ONE
Remove beige herringbone jacket
Remove rust belt
Remove Blue with pink stripe blouse with ribbon
Maroon plaid blouse with rust & blue bow
White pinafore
Grey cardigan sweater
ACT TWO, SCENE ONE
Remove grey cardigan sweater
ACT TWO, SCENE SIX
Remove maroon plaid blouse with rust & blue bow
Remove beige herringbone skirt
Remove white pinafore
Rust tweed dress with lace collar & cuffs
Ocre belt
"Heart" (taken off onstage)
Maroon cape
Reticule
ACT THREE
Remove maroon cape
Plaid shawl

MATTIE SILKS
ACT ONE, SCENE THREE
Corset with garters
Black stockings
Black petticoat
Black high-lace shoes
Mauve silk shell
Green skirt with black trim
Black Persian lamb jacket with fur trim
Black crochet gloves
Black hat with feathers
Black reticule & green drop earrings
ACT TWO, SCENE TWO
Remove mauve silk shell
Remove green skirt
Remove black Persian lamb jacket with fur trim
Remove black crochet gloves & black hat
Remove black reticule & green drop earrings.
Black & red evening dress
Red & black neck bow & gold chain
Black feather hair decoration
Black & silver drop earrings
ACT TWO, SCENE FIVE
Fur trimmed black cape
ACT TWO, SCENE NINE
Remove black & red evening dress
Remove red & black neck bow & gold chain
Remove black feather hair decoration
Black skirt
Brown brocade jacket
Black velvet belt & black & brown necklace

Black hat with feathers & reticule
ACT THREE
Remove fur-trimmed black cape

PIANIST
ACTS ONE — THREE
Burgundy dress with attached hip shawl
White petticoat
Dark pink mitts
Black velvet neck bow
Black feather hair decoration
Black stockings
Black lace-up shoes
ACT THREE
Black shawl

CHINESE WOMAN
Black cotton pants
Black top with frogs (layer 1)
Black cotton top (layer 2)
Black vest with gold—red stripe
Black quilted jacket
White V-neck T-shirt
2 pairs crew socks
Black high-top shoes
Black fabric square
Distressed stripe — legs & arms

WHORE / TOWNSPERSON / MOLLIE
ACT ONE, SCENE ONE
Pink corset & black stockings

Black lace-up shoes
White ruffled petticoat
Calico dress & red print apron
Straw hat & shawl
Wedding ring
White eyelet bloomers & garters
ACT ONE, SCENE THREE
Remove calico dress & red print apron
Remove straw hat & shawl
Black dress with jet trim
Brown cape coat & brown straw hat
Brown gloves
ACT ONE, SCENE FOUR
Remove brown cape coat & brown straw hat
Remove brown gloves
Black hat with black & blue bow
Black jet earrings
ACT ONE, SCENE FIVE
Remove black dress with jet trim
Remove white ruffled petticoat
Remove black hat with black & blue bow
Remove black jet earrings & wedding ring
Brown tweed cape
ACT TWO, SCENE TWO
Remove brown tweed cape
White ruffled petticoat
White organza dress
String of pearls
ACT TWO, SCENE FIVE
Remove white ruffled petticoat
Remove white organza dress

Remove string of pearls
Red & gold kimono
Brown tweed cape
ACT TWO, SCENE NINE
Remove red & gold kimono
Remove brown tweed cape
White ruffled petticoat
Green striped skirt & jacket
Brown straw hat & brown gloves
Wedding band
ACT THREE
Remove white ruffled petticoat
Remove green striped skirt & jacket
Remove brown straw hat & brown shawl
White with single ruffle petticoat
Blue & white striped blouse & skirt
Tan straw hat

WHORE / TOWNSPERSON
ACT ONE, SCENE ONE
Purple corset
Pink bloomers
Black stockings
Black lace-up stockings & garters
"Whore" petticoat
ACT ONE, SCENE TWO
Remove "whore" petticoat
White lace camisole
Petticoat with brown ruffle
Maroon skirt
Navy blouse

Plaid shawl
Wedding ring
ACT ONE, SCENE THREE
Remove maroon skirt
Remove navy blouse & plaid shawl
Black dress with lace trim
Black velvet belt
Brown carriage coat
Brown felt hat
ACT ONE, SCENE FOUR
Remove carriage coat
Remove brown felt hat
Black velvet & lace bonnet
Onyx earrings
ACT ONE, SCENE FOUR
Remove black dress with lace trim
Remove black velvet & lace bonnet
Remove onyx earrings & wedding ring
Remove brown petticoat & white lace camisole
Brown & black tweed cape
ACT TWO, SCENE TWO
Remove brown & black tweed cape
"Dance Hall" green & rust skirt
Green bodice
Black neck ribbon
"Whore" petticoat
Hair decoration
ACT TWO, SCENE FIVE
Remove "Dance Hall" green & rust skirt
Remove green bodice
Remove black neck ribbon

Remove "Whore" petticoat & hair decoration
White lace camisole
Brown & black tweed cape
Red & green kimono
ACT TWO, SCENE NINE
Remove brown & black tweed cape
Remove red & green kimono
Navy blouse
Brown petticoat
Maroon skirt
Brown carriage coat
Brown felt hat & brown shawl
Wedding ring
ACT THREE
Remove navy blouse
Remove maroon skirt
Remove brown carriage coat
Remove Brown felt hat & plaid shawl
Ocre blouse
Tan skirt
Tan straw hat

WHORE / TOWNSPERSON
ACT ONE, SCENE ONE
White corset
Purple bloomers
Off-white camisole
Black stockings & garters
Black lace-up shoes
Blue plaid jacket
Pink petticoat

Blue plaid skirt with ruffle
Wedding ring
ACT ONE, SCENE FIVE
Remove Blue plaid jacket
Remove blue plaid skirt with ruffle
Brown suit with black buttons
Blue checked underskirt
Black shawl & black hat
ACT TWO, SCENE TWO
Remove brown suit with black buttons
Remove blue checked underskirt
Remove black shawl & black hat
"Dance Hall" skirt with attached hip drape
Tan bodice
Green kimono
Feather hair decoration
ACT TWO, SCENE FIVE
Remove "Dance Hall" skirt with attached hip drape
Remove tan bodice
Remove green kimono
Remove feather hair decoration
Remove pink petticoat
Blue sheer camisole
Rust kimono & purple cape
ACT TWO, SCENE NINE
Remove blue sheer camisole
Remove rust kimono & purple cape
Brown suit with blue checked underskirt
Black hat & black shawl
Pink petticoat

ACT THREE
Remove brown suit with blue checked underskirt
Remove black hat & black shawl
Remove pink petticoat
Yellow calico dress with blue belt
Off-white straw hat

GEORGE WILDER
ACT ONE, SCENE ONE
Brown pants
Beige shirt
Brown striped vest
Spotted brown tie
Brown overcoat
Brown hat
Brown socks
Brown lace-up shoes
ACT ONE, SCENE FIVE
Remove overcoat
Suit coat
ACT ONE, SCENE EIGHT
Remove brown hat
ACT TWO, SCENE THREE
Remove suit coat
Overcoat
ACT TWO, SCENE NINE
Remove overcoat
Sportcoat
ACT THREE, SCENE ONE
Remove spotted brown tie
Striped brown tie

Hat (onstage)
Red armband on suit coat

MR. WHITMORE
ACT ONE, SCENE THREE
T-shirt / black socks
Beige striped shirt collar
Maroon tie
Charcoal trousers
Black vest with watch chain
Charcoal suit coat
Black high-top lace-up shoes
Vigilante duster & hood
ACT ONE, SCENE SIX
Overcoat
Black homberg
ACT ONE, SCENE EIGHT
Remove overcoat & hat
ACT TWO, SCENE FOUR
Hat
Overcoat
ACT THREE, SCENE ONE
Remove overcoat

SOAPY SMITH
ACT ONE, SCENE ONE
T-shirt & black socks
White shirt
Black pants
Black overcoat
Wide red & black stripe tie

Black lace-up shoes
Black hat
ACT ONE, SCENE FOUR A
Remove overcoat
Remove striped tie & black hat
Red silk smoking jacket
ACT ONE, SCENE FIVE
Remove smoking jacket
Vest with watch
Small red/black stripe tie
Suitcoat
ACT ONE, SCENE SIX
Black hat
ACT ONE, SCENE EIGHT
Remove hat
ACT TWO, SCENE ONE
Overcoat
ACT TWO, SCENE THREE
Remove overcoat
ACT TWO, SCENE FIVE
Remove suit coat
ACT TWO, SCENE NINE
Remove vest & tie
Remove white shirt & red striped tie
Remove black lace-up shoes
Black shirt
Same vest
Black boots
Black tie & hat
Suit coat

THE BALLAD OF SOAPY SMITH

ACT THREE, SCENE ONE
Remove black shirt & black tie
Remove black boots & black hat
Remove black vest
White shirt & paisley tie
Lace-up shoes
Same vest
Suitcoat

SYD DICKSON
ACT ONE, SCENE TWO
Dark gray pinstriped pants
Black socks / white T-shirt
Gray brocade vest with chain
Blue & red striped shirt with collar
Gray & red print bowtie
Floppy black hat
Leather coat (distressed)
ACT ONE, SCENE FIVE
Remove hat & coat
Dark gray pinstripe suit coat
Black fedora
Dark gray overcoat with velvet collar
ACT TWO, SCENE THREE
Remove overcoat
ACT THREE, SCENE THREE
Remove suit coat & collar
ACT THREE, SCENE SEVEN
Remove black fedora
Leather coat & floppy hat

ACT THREE, SCENE SEVEN
Remove leather coat & floppy hat
Black fedora

RUSSIAN JOHNNY / CORPORAL EGAN / ENSEMBLE
ACT ONE, SCENE THREE
T-shirt / black socks
Rust red shirt
Embroidered vest
Brown jersey pants
Black belt
Brown Persian lamb hat
Brown combat boots
ACT ONE, SCENE THREE
Remove rust red shirt
Remove embroidered vest
Remove brown jersey pants
Remove black belt & Persian lamb hat
Red thermal no-sleeve shirt
Plaid slacks with suspenders
Red checked coat
Distressed black cowboy hat
Same boots
ACT TWO, SCENE THREE
Remove thermal no-sleeve shirt
Remove plaid slacks with suspenders
Remove red checked coat & distressed black cowboy hat
Remove brown combat boots
Blue pants with suspenders
Blue cavalry shirt
Blue cavalry tunic

Blue cavalry overcoat
Cream gauntlet gloves
Beige muffler
Black cavalry hat
Black belt with holster & black cavalry boots
ACT THREE, SCENE TWO
Remove muffler, overcoat, tunic
Remove black hat & scarf
Brown military hat
ACT THREE, SCENE FIVE
Remove hat, gloves, boots
Remove belt with holster
Remove blue cavalry shirt with gold scarf
Remove pants with suspenders
Red thermal nosleeve shirt
Plaid slacks with suspenders
Blue checked coat
Distressed black cowboy hat
Same boots

PAUL ANTHONY McALEER
ACT ONE, SCENE ONE
T-shirt & black socks
Wallace Beery shirt
Checked "Cavalry" shirt
Brown-gray tweed pants
High-top black lace-up boots
Glasses
"Newspaper boy" cap
ACT ONE, SCENE SIX
Scarf & gloves

ACT ONE, SCENE EIGHT
Remove scarf & gloves
Apron (onstage)
ACT TWO, SCENE ONE
Remove checked shirt & apron
Remove brown-gray tweed pants
Off-white striped shirt with collar
Multicolor, 3-piece suit (with vest with watch fob)
Striped tie
ACT THREE, SCENE ONE
Red armband
ACT THREE, SCENE FIVE
Remove suit coat

REVEREND DICKEY
ACT ONE, SCENE SIX
T-shirt & black socks
Suit pants — gray-blue with suspenders
Black shirt with white collar
Gray sweater vest
Gray "miners" felt hat
ACT ONE, SCENE EIGHT
Remove hat & vest
Suitjacket with lapel pin
ACT TWO, SCENE ONE
Black overcoat
Hat (Act One, Scene Six)
ACT TWO. SCENE THREE
Remove overcoat & hat
Remove suitjacket with lapel pin
Remove gray-blue pants

Remove black shirt with white collar
Green shirt
Blue checked pants with suspenders
Brown checked vest
"Miners" hat (gray cowboy)
ACT TWO, SCENE NINE
Remove green shirt
Remove checked pants with suspenders
Remove brown checked vest
Remove "miners" hat (gray cowboy)
Suit pants
Black shirt with collar
Overcoat, black & gray
ACT THREE, SCENE ONE
Remove black & gray overcoat
Suit vest
Suit jacket
"Rev. Dickey" (Act One, Scene Six) hat

FRANK REID
ACT TWO, SCENE THREE
Brown heavy socks
Tweed pants with suspenders
Khaki shirt
Vigilante duster with hood
Brown high-lace boots
ACT ONE, SCENE EIGHT
Remove hood & duster
Red tie
Leather jacket

ACT TWO, SCENE ONE
Remove leather jacket
Remove red tie
Remove brown high-lace boots
Remove tweed pants with suspenders
Black shoes (lace-up)
3-piece multicolored suit
Brown tie
Brown overcoat
Brown cap
ACT TWO, SCENE THREE
Remove 3-piece suit
Remove brown tie
Remove overcoat
Remove black high-top shoes
Tweed pants
High lace-up boots
Brown cowboy hat
White gloves
ACT TWO, SCENE NINE
Remove overcoat & hat
Leather coat
ACT THREE, SCENE ONE
Remove leather coat
Hat
ACT THREE, SCENE FIVE
Leather coat

J.D. STEWART / ENSEMBLE
ACT ONE, SCENE THREE
T-shirt, black socks

Wallace Beery shirt
Yellow plaid shirt
Ripped brown / blue wool pants
Brown lace-up shoes
Distressed gray felt hat
ACT ONE, SCENE SIX
Brown plaid jacket
ACT TWO, SCENE THREE
Remove brown plaid jacket
Remove yellow flannel shirt
Remove Wallace Beery shirt
Remove ripped brown / blue wool pants
Remove brown lace-up shoes & gray hat
Light blue pants with suspenders
Dark blue tunic top
Blue coat with cape
Gold Neckerchief
Belt & holster
Black boots & black cavalry belt
ACT TWO, SCENE NINE
Remove cavalry
Wallace Beery shirt
Maroon flannel shirt
Ripped brown / blue pants
Brown jacket
Brown lace-up shoes
Distressed gray felt hat
ACT THREE, SCENE TWO
Remove ripped brown / blue pants
Remove brown jacket
Remove brown lace-up shoes

Remove gray felt hat
Rubber waist-high waders
Gloves
Reddish-plaid jacket
Brown cowboy hat

CLANCY / ENSEMBLE
ACT ONE, SCENE THREE A
Green shirt
Red necktie
Beige western hat
Brown Corduroy trousers
Tweed vest
Black lace-up ankle boots
T-shirt, black socks
ACT ONE, SCENE THREE
Remove hat
Vigilante duster & hood
ACT ONE, SCENE FOUR
Remove duster & hood
Brown jacket
Beige cowboy hat
ACT ONE, SCENE FIVE
Remove hat & jacket
ACT ONE SCENE SIX
Floppy hat
Long tweed coat
ACT ONE, SCENE EIGHT
Remove floppy hat & long tweed coat
Apron
ACT TWO, SCENE ONE
Remove apron, green shirt, red necktie

Remove brown corduroy trousers
Remove tweed vest & black lace-up ankle boots
Red union suit
ACT TWO, SCENE THREE
Black jodhpurs
Black riding boots
Blue cavalry tunic
Overcoat
Beige cavalry gloves
Black cavalry hat
ACT TWO, SCENE NINE
Remove cavalry overcoat
Remove cavalry tunic
Remove beige gloves & black cavalry hat
Gray tunic with red & gold trim
"Sam Brown" belt
Black "Mountie" hat
ACT THREE, SCENE ONE
Remove gray tunic with red & gold trim
Remove "Sam Brown" belt
Remove "Mountie" hat
Remove black jodhpurs
Remove black riding boots
Gray striped suit with watch chain on vest
Gray & black dot tie
Light brown shirt with celluloid collar
Brown felt hat
Black lace-up boots
ACT THREE, SCENE TWO A
Remove suit coat
Remove vest with watch chain

Remove striped shirt with celluloid collar
Red striped shirt
Tweed vest

JENSEN / ENSEMBLE
ACT ONE, SCENE THREE A
T-shirt & black socks
Beige long johns
Black & gray herringbone pants with suspenders
Gray turtleneck sweater
Brown pinstripe vest
Beige / yellow / brown plaid jacket
Distressed beige felt hat
Black ankle boots (lace up)
ACT ONE, SCENE THREE A
Remove plaid jacket
Remove distressed beige felt hat
Vigilante duster & hood
ACT ONE, SCENE FOUR A
Distressed beige felt hat
Beige / yellow / brown plaid jacket
ACT ONE, SCENE SIX
Remove coat & distressed hat
Remove gray T-neck sweater & vest
Grubby brown hat with blue braid
Brown corduroy coat
Gloves without fingers
ACT TWO, SCENE ONE
Remove corduroy coat, grubby brown hat & gloves
Red night shirt
Floppy hat over wig (loses hat on stage)

Big brown boots
ACT TWO, SCENE THREE
Remove red night shirt
Remove gray-black herringbone pants
Remove big brown boots
Black jodhpurs
Black riding boots
Blue tunic with kerchief attached
Blue overcoat/cape
Cavalry hat
Beige cavalry gloves
ACT TWO, SCENE NINE
Remove blue overcoat
Remove blue tunic with kerchief
Remove cavalry hat & beige cavalry gloves
Grey tunic with red & gold trim
"Sam Brown" belt
Black "Mountie" hat
ACT THREE, SCENE ONE
Remove black "Mountie" hat & "Sam Brown" belt
Remove gray with gold & red trim tunic
Remove black jodhpurs & black riding boots
Black & grey herringbone suit
Black ankle boots
Green & beige shirt with collar
Red cravat
Black vest with watch chain
Glasses
Olive derby
ACT THREE, SCENE TWO B
Remove olive derby

Remove shirt with collar
Remove black vest with watch chain
Remove suit coat
Remove glasses
Remove red cravat
Mustard yellow shirt with red stripes
Brown pin-stripe vest
Beige / yellow / brown plaid jacket
Distressed beige felt hat

TRIPOD: (BARITONE)   KLONDIKE GOLD (I, ii)

WORDS + MUSIC: MICHAEL WALLER
ARRANGEMENTS: NORMAN DURKEE

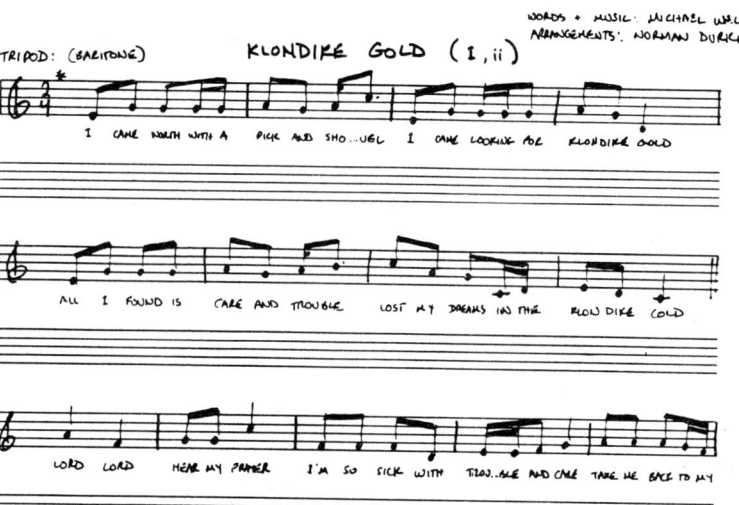

I came north with a pick and sho...vel I came looking for Klondike gold

All I found is care and trouble lost my dreams in the Klondike cold

Lord Lord hear my prayer I'm so sick with trouble and care take me back to my

wife and kin and I'll never go north for the gold a-gin.

* TRANSPOSE ALL SONGS TO COMFORTABLE KEY

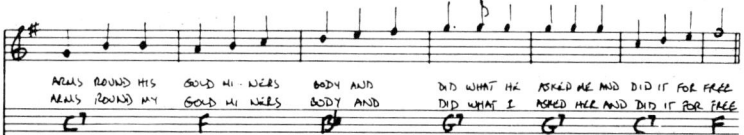

Other Publications for Your Interest

THE ROYAL HUNT OF THE SUN
(ALL GROUPS—HISTORY)
By PETER SHAFFER

22 men, 2 women—Cyc, drops, inset

The expedition of the Spanish under Pizzaro to the land of the Incas told in dazzling spectacle and moral chiaroscuro. After general absolution for any crimes they may commit against the pagan Incas, the conquerors set forth upon the sea. The Inca god is a sun god, ruler of the riches and people of Peru, and thought to be immortal. But the Spaniards have come in conquest rather than in reverence. There is a misunderstanding, confusion, and a slaughter in which the Spaniards kill 3000 unarmed and take the sun god captive. The ransom is 9000 pounds of gold. The avaricious Spaniards mutiny, try the sun god in kangaroo court, and then garrot him. He does not revive, and the Incas behold their dead god. "High intelligence and bold, imaginative reach . . . It has elements of the masque (and) pageant, soaring passages that recall the stage to its lofty enterprise, and a theme of enduring significance."—N.Y. Times. "Greatest play of our generation."—London Daily Mail.

(Royalty, $50-$25.)

BLACK COMEDY
(LITTLE THEATRE—FARCE)
By PETER SHAFFER

5 men, 3 women—Interior

Taking a page from the Chinese theatre, this farce opens on a dark stage (which is light to the characters), then blows a fuse throwing them all in the dark (which is light to the audience), and ends with lights reconnected (i.e., with a dark stage). What we see in the "dark" is this: A girl bringing her wealthy father to meet her fiance, an improvident sculptor, and to impress him, the sculptor has both invited a wealthy art patron and stolen the fine furniture from the apartment next door for his bare pad. Not only have the lights gone out, but everything else turns cockeyed—the neighbor returns too soon, the art patron is mistaken for an electrician, and a former flame pixies the proceedings from the bedroom. "Grand slapstick . . . Jolted me with laughter, and I was sorry indeed when the stage went dark and farce ended."—N.Y. Daily News. "A remarkably ingenious farce."—Wall Street Journal. "A truly hilarious and original farce . . . farcial situations and amusing characters that keep the hilarity spinning festively in the air."—N.Y. Post. "An evening with this uproarious play is like the rediscovery of laughter."—N.Y. World Journal Tribune. One of the biggest hits of the season and a perfect play for Little Theatre and College groups.

(Royalty, $50-$25.)

Other Publications for Your Interest

TALKING WITH...
(LITTLE THEATRE)
By JANE MARTIN

11 women—Bare stage

Here, at last, is the collection of eleven extraordinary monologues for eleven actresses which had them on their feet cheering at the famed Actors Theatre of Louisville—audiences, critics and, yes, even jaded theatre professionals. The mysteriously pseudonymous Jane Martin is truly a "find", a new writer with a wonderfully idiosyncratic style, whose characters alternately amuse, move and frighten us always, however, speaking to use from the depths of their souls. The characters include a baton twirler who has found God through twirling; a fundamentalist snake handler, an ex-rodeo rider crowded out of the life she has cherished by men in 3-piece suits who want her to dress up "like Minnie damn Mouse in a tutu"; an actress willing to go to any length to get a job; and an old woman who claims she once saw a man with "cerebral walrus" walk into a McDonald's and be healed by a Big Mac. "Eleven female monologues, of which half a dozen verge on brilliance."—London Guardian. "Whoever (Jane Martin) is, she's a writer with an original imagination."—Village Voice. "With Jane Martin, the monologue has taken on a new poetic form, intensive in its method and revelatory in its impact."—Philadelphia Inquirer. "A dramatist with an original voice...(these are) tales about enthusiasms that become obsessions, eccentric confessionals that levitate with religious symbolism and gladsome humor."—N.Y. Times. *Talking With...* is the 1982 winner of the American Theatre Critics Association Award for Best Regional Play. (#22009)

(Royalty, $60-$40.
If individual monologues are done separately: Royalty, $15-$10.)

HAROLD AND MAUDE
(ADVANCED GROUPS—COMEDY)
By COLIN HIGGINS

9 men, 8 women—Various settings

Yes: *the Harold and Maude!* This is a stage adaptation of the wonderful movie about the suicidal 19 year-old boy who finally learns how to truly *live* when he meets up with that delightfully whacky octogenarian, Maude. Harold is the proverbial Poor Little Rich Kid. His alienation has caused him to attempt suicide several times, though these attempts are more cries for attention than actual attempts. His peculiar attachment to Maude, whom he meets at a funeral (a mutual passion), is what saves him—and what captivates us. This new stage version, a hit in France directed by the internationally-renowned Jean-Louis Barrault, will certainly delight both afficionados of the film and new-comers to the story. "Offbeat upbeat comedy."—Christian Science Monitor. (#10032)

(Royalty, $60-$40.)

A Man for All Seasons
By ROBERT BOLT

DRAMA—2 ACTS—11 men, 3 women—Unit set

Garlands of awards and critical praise greeted this long-run success in both New York and London. In both productions Paul Scofield was pronounced brilliant for his portrayal of Sir Thomas More in his last years as Lord Chancellor of England during the reign of Henry VIII. When Henry failed to obtain from the Pope a divorce from Catherine of Aragon, in order to marry Anne Boleyn, he rebelled by requiring his subjects to sign an Act of Supremacy making him both spiritual and temporal leader of England. More could not in conscience comply. Neither Thomas Cromwell, nor Cardinal Wolsey nor the King himself could get a commitment from him. He resisted anything heroic; he wanted only to maintain his integrity and belief in silence. But this was treason, and his very silence led him to his death. " '*A Man For All Seasons*' is the ageless and inspiring echo of the small voice that calls to us: 'To thine own self be true.' . . . A smashing hit . . . A titantic hit . . . In conception and execution it is a masterpiece."—*N. Y. Journal-American*.

(Royalty, $50-$25.)

J. B.
By ARCHIBALD MacLEISH

VERSE DRAMA—2 ACTS
12 men, 9 women—Interior

Winner of the Pulitzer Prize for playwriting

The following is from the review of *J. B.* by Brooks Atkinson in the *New York Times:* "Looking around at the wreckage and misery of the modern world, Mr. MacLeish has written a fresh and exalting morality that has great stature. In an inspired performance yesterday evening, it seemed to me one of the memorable works of the century as verse, as drama and as spiritual inquiry. The stage is set . . . in the form of a circus tent . . . Two circus peddlers make whimsical use of the tent by playing God and the Devil. Presently we are deep in the unanswered problems of man's relationship to God in an era of cruel injustices. J. B., a modern business man rich with blessings, is Mr. MacLeish's counterpart of the immortal Job . . . J. B. is brought down by the terrible affliction of our century—deaths and violent catastrophes that seem to have no cause or meaning . . . The glory of Mr. MacLeish's play is that, as in the Book of Job, J. B. does not curse God. When he is reunited with his wife, two humbled but valiant people accept the universe, agree to begin life over again, expecting no justice but unswerving in their devotion to God.

(Royalty, $50-$25.)

PS 3573 .E457 B35 1985

Weller, Michael, 1942-

The ballad of Soapy Smith